Solzhenitsyn
and the Secret Circle

Also by Olga Carlisle

Voices in the Snow
Poets on Street Corners

SOLZHENITSYN
AND THE SECRET CIRCLE

Olga Carlisle

HOLT, RINEHART and WINSTON

New York

Published simultaneously in Canada by Holt, Rinehart and
Winston of Canada, Limited.

Library of Congress Cataloging in Publication Data

Carlisle, Olga Andreyev.
Solzhenitsyn and the secret circle.

1.   Solzhenitsyn, Aleksandr Isaevich, 1918–
—Friends and associates.   2.   Carlisle, Olga Andreyev.
3.   Authors, Russian—20th century—Biography.
I.   Title.
PG3488.04Z593   891.7'3'44   77–20216
ISBN 0–03–040696–X

*The lines from Feydor Tyutchev's "Cicero" and from Sergei
Yessenin's "The Bent Streets of Moscow" were adapted by
W. S. Merwin with Olga Carlisle. The lines from Boris
Pasternak's "False Alarm" were adapted by Robert Lowell
with Olga Carlisle. The lines from Andrei Voznesensky's
"New York Airport at Night" were adapted by Henry
Carlisle. All appeared in* Poets on Street Corners.

FIRST EDITION

Designer: Joy Chu

Printed in the United States of America
1 2 3 4 5 6 7 8 9 10

To Michael

I wish to express my appreciation to many people in Russia and in Europe who cannot be named in this book. For their support, my thanks to Marian Wood, and to Marie-Luise Hirsch; and also to my husband, Henry Carlisle, without whom there would have been no secret circle.

When the state tore at itself in agony
Rome's orator said, "I got up
too late and the night of Rome overtook me
on the way." Maybe,
but as you bade farewell to Rome's glory
you beheld from the Capitoline Hill
her bloody star
setting in full majesty.

Blessed is he
whose visit to the world has fallen
in its moments of destiny.
The kind powers have welcomed him
to their banquet, to converse as an equal. He
sees the striding glories that they see,
he has a place at their councils, he drinks
from their own cup immortality,
in his time he lives as they do in heaven.

—Feydor Tyutchev
"Cicero"

Contents

ONE

Night Walk in Moscow

WE WALKED down a street that was completely deserted. I was very cold. I could feel Solzhenitsyn's rage in his tightening hold on my arm. Our steps echoed down that dark, empty Moscow street. Then he spoke, and what he said left me limp, even as his own movements became more charged with energy. Alexander Solzhenitsyn was asking me to take charge of the publication in the West of the novel the KGB had "arrested." It was called *The First Circle*.

That was in April 1967, when the long Cold War between the Soviet Union and the West appeared to be thawing.

When I think back to Moscow in that spring, I recall with photographic clarity the section of the city between Red Square and the Leningradskaya Hotel, to the northeast. It was a district I had often walked through, varying my route a bit each time, following one or another of the crooked lanes which meet each other at odd angles. This part of town still had a feeling of old Moscow, when the city was a colorful, semi-Asiatic marketplace. By day, it was full of life, crowded with shoppers from the country, women in heavy navy blue coats and knitted gray kerchiefs, leading bundled children by the hand; men in ancient sheepskin coats; peasants carrying birds in homemade cages headed for the pet market nearby; peddlers offering thread and shoelaces for sale; a smell of cabbage drifting in the air. Each lane had its own unexpected angle, its randomly placed little stucco houses, with diminutive gardens behind plank fences. Painted in shades of ocher and pink, these houses had once been owned by Moscow merchants. People still lived in them. Geraniums and rubber plants grew behind lace curtains. Logs stood neatly stacked in the courtyards. All day long the little shops and eating places were full of clanging activity until, around six, the district would suddenly fall silent for the night.

I took many walks through those ancient side streets that spring. The one with Alexander Solzhenitsyn was to change my life.

THIS VISIT to Moscow was my fourth. I was in Russia gathering material for an anthology of contemporary Soviet poetry, a book I had been at work on for almost five years. As on previous visits, I saw many people, made new acquaintances, called on elderly relatives and friends of my family. These old-time intellectuals, some of whom had returned from labor camps not long before, subsisted on tiny pensions, poetry, and hope. Some had known my paternal grandfather, the writer Leonid Andreyev. They gave me tea and kulich, the traditional Easter cake. In one-room apartments, full of books, drawings, modest treasures from the past, they would quote lines of Pasternak celebrating love and springtime. They assured me that things would continue to improve in Russia. Back in the fifties, they said, who would have believed that I, a Paris-born Russian now living in the United States, would be allowed to visit them in Moscow? That books by Pasternak and Marina Tsvetayeva could appear in the Soviet Union and that Solzhenitsyn's *Cancer Ward* would, they had heard, soon be published? That we would have kulich for tea? I wanted to share their hope—I loved them very much. I wanted to believe that Moscow was, after all, my home; for, outside of my immediate family, some of the people to whom I felt closest lived there.

But that spring there were signs this Russia of common memories and hopes was neither mine nor theirs.

EARLY IN THAT VISIT friends arranged for me to meet the poet Joseph Brodsky. It had been a difficult evening. Brodsky had sulked demonstratively while my friends tried in vain to bring him out. When he did speak, it was to praise President Johnson for escalating the war in Vietnam. Only later, when he read his poems, did the atmosphere grow less tense. As I left, the poet gave me one of his poems in typescript with the handwritten words "From Russia with love."

That evening as I left my friends and the poet, I felt a deep uneasiness. The apartment was near the Kremlin. Returning to the Leningradskaya I first followed the Kremlin's outer fortifications on the Manège side. It had snowed lightly the day before and the crenellated outlines of the ramparts were etched with fine white. When I turned into a side street leading in the direction of my hotel, I saw that, since morning, one of my favorite clusters of old houses had been bulldozed to rubble. In the dusk, a city block of six or seven small town houses was now a low mound of pinkish debris flecked with white plaster and broken bricks. The air tasted of dust. Where, I wondered, had the oc-cupants of these houses gone? I was shaken. What was I doing in this treacherous city, whose most picturesque old section was being destroyed even as I was still discovering it? Where an inspired young poet could praise Americans for bombing Vietnam? As I passed the pink rubble, Sergei Yessenin's menacing lines came to my mind:

> *The golden somnolence of Asia*
> *Dozes on the cupolas. . . .*
> *I know God means I am to die*
> *Among the bent streets of Moscow.*

I wanted to leave the city, to go home at once. At that moment my efforts at opening lines of communication between Russian and Western intellectuals seemed ridiculous, presumptuous, a delusion. Shaped by lifetimes of isolation and anger, most younger Soviet intellectuals would not hear points of view other than their own, which they felt were sanctified by their suffering. As the older generation faded away, the spiritual break between past and present, East and West, could only widen.

I entered the opulent, blood-red interior of the Leningradskaya in anguish.

The next morning I woke in a more collected frame of mind. I still wanted to start home ahead of schedule, but something stopped me from changing my ticket. I thought of all the things I had yet to do in Moscow: appointments to keep, relatives to visit, medicines and packages to deliver to friends and friends of friends. I decided to stay.

One of the people I cared most for in Moscow was the critic and writer of children's stories Kornei Chukovsky. It was he who would play a crucial role in bringing about my meeting with Alexander Solzhenitsyn.

DAYS WENT BY and spring weather continued to elude Moscow. I shivered in my Western winter clothing. In previous Aprils when I had visited the city, budding leaves had dusted the trees with green, the outdoor markets were massed with bunches of wild flowers. The young poets of Moscow, Andrei Voznesensky,

Yevgeny Yevtushenko, and Bella Akhmadulina, had proclaimed the dawn of a new era in Russian life. This thaw of the early sixties had brought forth fresh feelings and new works of art in Russia. But by 1967 the younger Muscovites had lost their ebullience; my friends among the young poets were apprehensive and depressed—none so deeply as the most fiery of them all, Yevtushenko.

The poet and his wife asked me to drop by their apartment. Yevtushenko was resting at home between "demanding, triumphal worldwide voyages," as he described them over the phone. I arrived to find him stretched out on a couch in the living room, undergoing an acupuncture session. With sudden rapid movements, a diminutive Chinese man was shifting long golden needles from one spot to another in Yevtushenko's torso. His wife, Galya, was sitting nearby, knitting. Almost at once the poet began to describe in a low monotone the persecutions he was being subjected to at the hands of literary officials. I saw that he was sick and suffering from depression. He said that freedom was again being crushed in Russia: that the authorities were conducting a cunning, systematic silencing of liberals, the very people who were still speaking to visiting Westerners in what they believed was relative safety. At this, Galya dropped her knitting to her lap and pointed to the ceiling. Yevtushenko lowered his voice even more. The authorities were increasingly active, he said. No one could escape this silent, relentless wave of repression. Not even he. Despite his conciliatory attitude toward the Writers Union, he was experiencing his share of petty humiliations.

With the long, shimmering, golden needles sticking out of his chest he resembled a Renaissance St. Sebastian.

Sadly I recalled the proud, flamboyant Yevtushenko of the early sixties, the messenger to the world of Soviet cultural reawakening. I remembered, too, the Yevtushenko I had seen in New York only a few months before. The occasion was his meeting with Robert Kennedy. In the company of various Kennedy friends and aides, I had acted as interpreter. One statement of Yevtushenko's had surprised me, so much so that I must have faltered, fighting a desire to amend it. (The senator, I believe, noticed this, observing with humor that whoever I was, I was not a professional interpreter.) It was Yevtushenko's claim that the thaw in Russia had been heralded by two literary works: *One Day in the Life of Ivan Denisovich* by Alexander Solzhenitsyn and "The Heirs of Stalin" by Yevgeny Yevtushenko. I had been surprised that Yevtushenko would set his own short poem alongside the novella that had been viewed in Russia as a rocket illuminating the somber world of the Soviet prison system and signaling a new liberalization of Soviet literature.

That spring of 1967 everyone in Moscow was talking about Alexander Solzhenitsyn. There were endless speculations about the legendary former *zek* (as Soviet prisoners are called), now a teacher of mathematics in the provincial town of Ryazan. Since the publication of *One Day*, many thoughtful Russians had been determined to make their history and their fears for the future known to the world. However, in the sixties, an open call for sympathy and support from public opinion outside of Russia would have been repugnant to most. Not only would it have seemed unpatriotic, it also could have been dangerous. What was needed was a literature at once truthful and bold enough to carry the message of Russian liberals outside the USSR. Solzhenitsyn was being looked to as the one person who might, through his art, make the Russian experience known to the world.

When I left the Yevtushenkos that afternoon I was aware that Solzhenitsyn's name had not once been mentioned.

I HAD NEVER MET Solzhenitsyn. I knew that he had admired my father's book about my grandfather, Leonid Andreyev. That spring, people often asked whether as a journalist I was not tempted to try to meet the author of *One Day*. Everyone knew I was a journalist; I took pains to make clear my reasons for being in Moscow, so as not to compromise anyone who wished to avoid Western journalists. Until recently, the average Russian had been terrified of foreigners, especially foreign journalists. For some, this fear was now giving way to the desire to meet these reporters and writers, who were viewed as potentially protective links with the West. Solzhenitsyn, however, avoided all journalists in those years, especially foreign ones; and though we had a close friend in common, Chukovsky, my chances of meeting the new star of Russian letters seemed small. Yes, I said, of course I wanted to meet him, but since my time in Moscow was running out, and since I still had work to do and people to see in connection with my book, I was not going out of my way to seek an encounter which was unlikely ever to come about.

I WAS CLOSE to my departure date and had set the day aside for packing. It would not be an easy undertaking. Though I always gave some of my clothes to Moscow friends before I left, their generosity far exceeded mine, and with innumerable presents to pack—books, records, some marvelous Ukrainian painted plaster figures—and the materials I had collected for the poetry book, my suitcase would as usual be too small for everything.

And was it a good idea to carry manuscripts through customs on this trip? There was, for instance, the complete transcript of Alexander Galich's irreverent, lyrical ballads, which Kornei Chukovsky had just given me. They were then the rage of Moscow and Kornei Ivanovich told me that they were masterpieces of Soviet vernacular and had to be represented in my book. But how to get them out? Galich was an underground poet-singer, a dissenter, and the chances of my luggage being searched were excellent.

I was debating such questions when the telephone rang.

It was an acquaintance, asking me to a small party the following night. L. and his wife had a rare surprise for me. From the tone of his voice I knew that someone I might want to meet would be there and I guessed that it might be the writer all Moscow was talking about. He hung up quickly. Exhilarated at the prospect of such an encounter, a final gift from Moscow before my departure, and the thought of returning home giving me wings, I decided to take a last walk in my favorite streets, postponing the job of packing until that afternoon.

An hour later I was returning to the Leningradskaya along a crooked street, my elation waning in the lusterless damp midday. I would be leaving Moscow without having seen the iridescent bluish light which in other springs had illuminated the city as if from within. Instead, Moscow was afloat with gigantic propaganda placards celebrating the approaching fiftieth anniversary of the October coup d'état. They were everywhere. They made the city seem like an obsessive dream.

When I approached my room I found that the door was ajar. Two men in blue overalls stood in the middle of the room, in some confusion. My approaching steps had pulled them away from whatever they had been doing. They held screwdrivers. As I entered I asked them why they were there. Fixing the plumbing, one told me. Before I could ask why they were fixing plumbing in the bedroom, near the telephone, and using screwdrivers instead of wrenches, they hurriedly disappeared out the door, two blue shadows vanishing into the gray Moscow noon.

Now I was swept by that outraged sense one feels when one's privacy is violated, as after a burglary. I stood at the window, looking down from my upper floor at the Plaza of the Three Railway Stations, at the intersecting tramway tracks on the pavement, the pattern of train tracks beyond, some freight cars pulling by very slowly. To my left lay the old part of Moscow, where I had just walked; part of it was being torn down to make way for a new thoroughfare. Across the plaza, a gigantic poster of Lenin in snap-brim cap was being raised to celebrate the Glorious October. As it was maneuvered into place the extended arm seemed to jerk menacingly in my direction.

The telephone rang and, still studying the melancholy cityscape, the surrealistic Lenin, wishing I were on my way home, I answered it.

The T.s were a couple I knew only slightly. Now the husband was speaking in a careful, urgent voice. Would I come to their apartment the following morning at ten? It was a matter of importance. Someone would be there. Again the tone of voice and the carefully chosen words telegraphed a coded message that the someone could be from Ryazan. Thinking of the men in blue, I was grateful that T. was cautious. I said I would be there at ten, then hung up immediately.

Two invitations for the same day. Two guarded yet excited callers. Solzhenitsyn saw almost no one from the West. The T.s were Communist party members. They were fully aware that I was an occasional contributor to the *New York Times* book section, to the *Saturday Evening Post* and *L'Express*. If I was right in my guess that I was about to meet Solzhenitsyn, then the invitations had to have been issued with his consent. Yet, as I thought about the calls, it never occurred to me that anything more than an exceptionally interesting encounter might be involved.

Many years, crowded with events that flowed from the next morning's meeting, have passed and my impression of it while strong, is not clear in all details. I remember it was another chilly day. Arriving at the T.s' apartment in the center of town, I started up a dark, drafty staircase with pairs of apartments at each landing, the black doors showing no names, the numbers often missing or with digits torn off—an inheritance from the era of fear when everyone in Russia tried to hide his identity. But this was 1967, and I walked up the rough concrete stairway with a light step. I must have reached the second or third floor when I became aware of someone descending. In the dark stairway above, a man appeared and for a second looked at me intently, then abruptly averted his eyes, passed by me, and darted downstairs. He wore a hat—I think it was a navy blue beret—and I recall that he carried a small rucksack on his back, a common sight in Moscow, where shopping for daily necessities is a time-consuming, complicated affair. I was conscious of a sharp, elongated face, that brief searching glance, and the furtive intensity of his movements. That intensity and his evident desire not to be identified made me think that perhaps this was indeed the author of *One Day*, the former *zek*. I went on up to the apartment and was ringing the bell when the sharp-faced man returned upstairs with rapid steps and stood beside me before the T.s' door. He looked at me and smiled, and at that moment I was certain he was Solzhenitsyn.

We went in together and were received warmly by the T.s and introduced to each other. We all shook hands. Clearly the writer was a good friend of my hosts. In the light of the apartment, I saw that Solzhenitsyn had reddish blond hair and that he was full of good health and alertness. I remember noting the difference between his fitness and the run-down appearance of some of his Moscow admirers who led harried lives, smoking and drinking until late at night, discussing the future of Russia.

Studying me attentively, Alexander Solzhenitsyn said a few cordial words about our mutual friend Chukovsky, then turned his attention to others in the room, the T.s and a young man whose name I could not recall but whose face was familiar to me. I knew I had seen him over the years at Moscow poetry readings.

I sat down in a corner of the square and rather impersonal room. Mrs. T. was not much concerned with her apartment, perhaps because she had a successful academic career and was away from home a great deal. There was a table in the middle of the room which evidently did double duty as a dining table and as a desk—one end of it was piled high with books and typewritten manuscripts. The T.s and their two other guests settled in chairs around the table while I sat a bit to the side on a couch. Across the room I noticed a large photograph of the poet Anna Akhmatova in her old age, as I had known her when we met a few years before, majestic and still beautiful. Her presence there was reassuring.

I was absorbed by what I saw and heard. This was a milieu I was not familiar with—that of anti-Stalinist party members and nonparty sympathizers, some of whom had served labor camp sentences under Stalin and still kept their political faith intact. In previous years the liberal intelligentsia of Moscow had pinned its hopes on these people, best exemplified by Alexander Tvardovsky, eminent poet and editor of Russia's best literary journal,

Novi Mir. Now the intelligentsia was becoming disenchanted with them for their inability to forestall reaction. I was wondering whether Solzhenitsyn, though not himself a party member, was politically allied with them. I had always assumed that he was, yet something in his manner now told me that he was of another world altogether. He seemed much shrewder and less vulnerable than the rest of the company.

They were discussing the possible publication of *Cancer Ward* in *Novi Mir.* I could not follow the conversation very well because Solzhenitsyn's works were not referred to by title but by abbreviated nicknames—or perhaps they were code names; but here and there I could catch a reference, and I was fascinated. As the conversation livened I wondered fleetingly why I had been invited. That year, my husband and I were completing a new translation of Dostoyevsky's *The Idiot*, and, as I sat and listened, I thought of those unforgettable encounter scenes in the novel, when characters meet unexpectedly in parlors or on park benches to discuss in cryptic tones some philosophical fancy or earth-shaking "scandal" about to break out.

T. and the young man whose name I could not remember were quite agitated—they acted as if they were in the presence of a man they truly revered. Each seemed to want to persuade Solzhenitsyn that a given strategy aimed at facilitating the publication of his work in Soviet magazines was the correct one. Both were anxious to help and offered to make use of their connections. He was listening to them, saying little while each man in turn spoke. He seemed intrigued but remained evasive: his ascendancy over the others was striking.

Glancing at Akhmatova's picture, I suddenly remembered a story about Solzhenitsyn and Akhmatova which Chukovsky had told me. Shortly before *One Day* was published, its author had given it to Akhmatova to read along with some poetry he had written in camp. Akhmatova told him: "You have such a high gift for prose—why would you want to compete with us poets? As for *One Day*, it will make you famous. Now the question is: Are you ready for fame?"

She had, of course, been right. He had become a celebrity in Russia, though circumstances were such that his had to be an underground kind of fame. Once again I thought of Dostoyevsky, of his characters coming together in secret to promote some subterranean, explosive cause.

After about forty minutes, the young man said good-bye and left. I sensed that it was also time for me to go. As I was taking leave, Solzhenitsyn took me aside and said, "I knew who you were when I saw you on the stairs. From your photograph in Chukovsky's study. For a time I worked every day in that study. Kornei Ivanovich has been good to me in difficult times."

He did not mention that we might be seeing each other again at the L.s', nor did I.

IN CONTRAST WITH the T.s' apartment, the L.s' was filled with paintings and drawings. Above a couch covered with a worn oriental rug, a collection of Moscow underground art was displayed. As usual, the effect of these surrealistic works was at first old-fashioned. Upon closer scrutiny, the intensity with which those pictures had been created transcended the predictability of their forms and made them absorbing—a symbolic, dark vision of the closed world in which Russian intellectuals live. We sat on the couch under the paintings. A narrow table before us was loaded with teacups, wineglasses, and modest snacks. Tea and wine were served throughout the evening.

The atmosphere here was very different from the T.s', the conversation much more candid and hushed. Solzhenitsyn's presence made this evening's gathering a special occasion. He seemed a different person here, more outspoken than at the T.s'. Here too he dominated the gathering, yet each person in this group of independent-spirited Muscovites had his own viewpoint and would not be swayed or silenced. Solzhenitsyn listened with particular attention to one of the guests, a man I knew to be a distinguished scientist. Solzhenitsyn was a gifted listener. His powers of absorption and retention of what others had to say were striking, and I realized even then that they must be an important element of his literary talent.

In the early part of that evening, Solzhenitsyn was expounding on how ineffectual the Socialist Revolutionaries had been before and after the February Revolution of 1917.

"What ineptitude! To think that in the summer of 1917 they had let Lenin go into hiding in the countryside of Finland! The more I look into the history of that era, the more appalled I am by how divorced from reality they all were. All the empty speeches."

As he spoke his eyes fell on me. My maternal grandfather had been a leading member of the Socialist Revolutionaries, the group that had dominated the provisional government until it was overthrown by the October coup d'état. Why had they not arrested Lenin after the Bolsheviks' first attempt to seize power by force in July 1917? Why had they all been so meek, so lost in debate and empty speeches?

I knew that Solzhenitsyn was right—the Socialist Revolutionaries had failed as leaders of the provisional government, which for a brief time during World War I had offered hope for true constitutional democracy in Russia. "Their political failure," I told him, "was inevitable from the start. The Socialist Revolutionaries had no aptitude for power. They were idealists brought up on concepts from the Age of Enlightenment. They had squandered the precious time circumstances had granted them in arguments. They were too scrupulous to withdraw Russia's armies from the Allied forces. Moreover, isn't it a common pattern of revolutions that moderates start them and radicals finish them?"

Solzhenitsyn listened, intrigued perhaps to be hearing these views from a granddaughter of Victor Chernov. He said he agreed, asked questions, pressed other points, and soon the conversation took another direction.

I was impressed by Solzhenitsyn. In company such as this he was most engaging—witty and self-assured without being overbearing. He seemed to enjoy himself thoroughly. He could listen with an affable smile to someone's rather predictable indictment of the Socialist Revolutionaries' political blunders. He could spellbind the gathering as he talked about the likelihood of Stalin's having been a double agent of the tsarist secret police before the Revolution. I was impressed by the rigorousness of his mind and by his rich, idiosyncratic speech. This was not the lyrical Russian I had heard from older Russian writers, from Alexei Remizov or Boris Pasternak. Alexander Solzhenitsyn's was an altogether different tongue. It was Soviet Russian, robust, staccato, with a modern vernacular unfamiliar to me, now and then an ancient folk proverb from the depths of rural Russia, and occasional prison camp terms which, though I did not understand them very well, touched me as I heard them for the first time in his intense, high-pitched voice. The *zek* expressions reminded me of his strength, of his ability to survive Stalin's concentration camps in order to tell the world about them. I could now see for myself why so many in Moscow that spring looked upon this man as a true Russian hero.

We left the apartment at the same time and, as I was about to hail a taxi, Solzhenitsyn offered to walk me back to the Leningradskaya, a considerable distance across town. I accepted. We started down a dimly lit side street. I remember remarking that this was the section of Moscow where half a century before my mother and her Socialist Revolutionary family had for a time lived in hiding after the October Revolution. To this, Solzhenitsyn made no response. As we walked we talked about Chukovsky, about the study where Solzhenitsyn had worked, with its windows looking out onto fir trees, a room for concentrated literary labors. He spoke of the photograph of me, saying it had helped him write. "You looked so serious, so stern," he said, adding with a trace of regret, "You're not as stern as I'd imagined."

The dark streets were icy and Solzhenitsyn offered me his arm. I was aware of his physical strength, of the spring of his step. His face showed his age, just under fifty, but his walk was that of a much younger person. It was hard to believe, as did most Muscovites from the evidence of *Cancer Ward*, that this man had almost died of cancer more than ten years before.

Then, as we walked, Solzhenitsyn told me about his war with the Soviet secret police. The KGB, he said, was out to destroy him. They would never forgive him for *One Day*, which had caused a wave of popular feeling that might well have engulfed state security. Some months before, they had "arrested"—this was the KGB's term—the manuscript of a novel of his which, along with other literary materials, he had entrusted for safe-keeping to a friend in Moscow. Suddenly he was full of rage. "What sort of country is this, where a *book* can be arrested?" he demanded. Now his enemies were having it printed in a private limited edition destined to discredit him in Soviet official circles, especially among those who decide what will and what will not be published. This novel, written before *Cancer Ward* and considered seditious, was about a special prison in Moscow in the late nineteen forties.

Now Tvardovsky, despite his promises, was proving incapable of publishing *Cancer Ward* in *Novi Mir*. Solzhenitsyn spoke scathingly about Tvardovsky, calling him a drunkard. Earlier in the evening, he had attacked Tvardovsky, though in more restrained language. Then, his words had astonished me. Like many Western readers of *One Day* who knew something of the story of its publication, of Tvardovsky's central role in bringing it to Khrushchev's attention, I had assumed that author and editor were friends.

As for his own situation, what people were saying was true: At home in Ryazan he was hounded by thugs in the pay of the KGB. They spied on him, threw stones at his house, tried to terrify him and his family. They were relentless.

We walked on, down the empty streets. I was cold. Slowing his pace, Solzhenitsyn told me that the *Cancer Ward* affair was all over now, at least as far as *Novi Mir* was concerned. Now this new novel, which was all over Moscow in *samizdat*—illegal, secretly copied versions—was unlikely to be officially published in the USSR for a very long time. However an extraordinary occurrence, an act of God, had just taken place. Only a few days before, a group of Yugoslav journalists had somehow made their way to Ryazan to interview him, despite all obstacles set up by the Writers Union, which was determined to isolate the author of *One Day*. He had given a manuscript of *Cancer Ward* to one of them. This was a dangerous act, but he had no choice. The KGB was tightening its noose. Anti-Stalinist party members were now impotent against the reactionary elements within the Soviet government. Tvardovsky was powerless, unable to help him anymore in his mission to make known to Russians and to the world the magnitude of the crimes committed by Stalin in the name of the Communist party. The possibility of a dreadful, irreparable failure loomed before him.

I could feel Solzhenitsyn's anger as he gripped my arm. For a moment he was silent. I still remember the echo of our steps in the street. Then he said, "I want you to see to the publication of *The First Circle* in the West."

I suddenly felt limp. I had by now half guessed that our meetings that day had not altogether happened by chance. My presence in Russia and his immediate need to have *The First Circle* published abroad had appeared to him as more than a coincidence: it was almost a sign. From Chukovsky he knew about my Russian background and of my work as a journalist writing about Soviet art and literature. He also knew from Chukovsky that my husband was a former book editor, experienced in publishing. He knew that we had done translations together. The time had come for him to publish his major work, a work the Soviet authorities considered subversive. The time had come to publish *The First Circle*—in the West, since it could not appear in Russia.

I was to arrange for the translation and publication of the novel in such a way as to draw as much attention to it as possible. "Let it stun public opinion throughout the world," he said. "Let the true nature of these scoundrels be known."

I remember the cold, and the sharpness of Solzhenitsyn's face in the faint light of a distant street lamp. We had stopped. Releasing my arm, he searched my face, wanting to know whether

I had fully understood. I had. The responsibility for me and the danger to him froze my blood. So did the feeling of fatality, the feeling that this moment was the culmination not only of this phantasmagoric day but of my life to that moment. I had been trapped by Yessenin's menacing bent streets after all. Around us as we walked, the curved dreamlike alleys formed a dark web.

He told me then that *The First Circle* was his most important book, the one that mattered, the one that would strike at the core of the Soviet leadership.

"A big book—my life," he said, and then: "Of course, it will have to be done in absolute secrecy. You can imagine what would happen to me if you were found out."

I knew very well, for nothing at that moment so awed me as the knowledge that he was putting his safety—his freedom and perhaps his life—into my hands. And it was a mission he set at a higher value than his life. Nothing then mattered to me so much as that, nor would for years to come.

Yet I also realized that, in a different way, irretrievably, I was at that moment losing part of my freedom too; that sooner or later, if I agreed to do what Solzhenitsyn was asking, I would lose touch with Russian relatives and friends, with the country of my parents' birth, which I had discovered and which had already become like another homeland, as much mine as the West. Still, it did not occur to me that I could say no, nor did it, I believe, to him. I told him that I would do the best I could.

At once, with intense excitement at the prospect of the battle ahead, Solzhenitsyn began to outline his overall plan of action in his duel with the Soviet establishment. I was learning that Solzhenitsyn planned his actions with the imagination of a great military leader, using military terms to describe them. He spoke of salvos and explosions. As we walked on slowly toward the hotel, words flew between us. My questions, his precise, exalted responses. In a few weeks, during the International Writers Conference to be held in Moscow as part of the fiftieth-anniversary celebration, he would issue a statement. It would be an unprecedented event, it would rock the Soviet literary establishment. Would I see that it was reported as amply as possible in the West? I said that I would do what I could.

We came into view of the block of leveled rubble that had so disturbed me earlier in my visit. I was trying to engrave in my mind, in his exact words, all that Solzhenitsyn was telling me. Suddenly I felt that I needed a moment to breathe. For just a moment, to have some contact with the man beside me that had nothing to do with the awesome undertaking before us. When he paused for an instant, I called his attention to the reddish rubble. "Old Moscow is being destroyed," I said. He barely nodded in acknowledgment—and went on without further pause, setting forth his strategies. It was not the destruction of a few old buildings that could matter to him at that moment, but the enlightenment of an entire generation of Russians. Nor could he welcome a show of sentimentality from the "stern" woman he had chosen to act for him.

Soon we were near the hotel, with its police spies shepherding the foreign guests. There was no more time. There could be no other meeting. We shook hands and Solzhenitsyn disappeared down a side street.

Then, for some reason I cannot fully explain even now, I started running toward the hotel. Hardly knowing what I was doing, I followed the edge of the dimly lit expanse of the Plaza of the Three Railroad Stations. Then, abruptly, I realized that I was running and forced myself to slow my steps. From now on I could do nothing that might attract attention.

2

Leaving the Leningradskaya for the airport on the icy April day of my departure, I carried not a single written word that could have linked me to Alexander Solzhenitsyn. I carried with me only my intense impressions of what had passed between us. Yet an hour later when I entered the customs area at Sheremetyevo, I could imagine that the uniformed customs men and women, and the plainclothes KGB, might somehow be trained to read the minds of departing travelers for just such secrets as I was bearing out of Russia.

I did have with me other literary materials I knew could arouse suspicion and create difficulties. In a pocket of my skirt, under my sheepskin coat, I carried the notebook with transcribed poems and notes for my anthology. And behind the stiff lining of my large black leather purse, I had stuffed the onionskin sheets, given to me by Chukovsky, on which the ballads by Galich were typed.

I had been troubled about the Galich ballads; they posed more of a risk than my poetry notes, which I kept cryptic. I knew that I must not take chances that could draw attention to me and perhaps impair my ability to carry out Solzhenitsyn's request. Because of my many known contacts with other Soviet writers and artists, it was possible that I would be searched, and I knew that I should dispose of the ballads; but that morning, remembering with what impetuous joy Chukovsky had recited some of these songs, I could not bear to tear them up and flush them down the toilet. Now, behind the lining of my bag, they felt like tablets of lead as I entered the airport.

I checked in at the very last minute, hoping that if a search was planned it would not be a thorough one. I knew that taking a passenger off a flight was an extreme measure not often resorted to.

As it happened, the calculation worked. I was met by a disagreeable pale-haired, rat-faced young man, decidedly upset by my tardiness. Hurriedly, half screened by a glass partition, he and another man opened and searched roughly through my suitcase, emptied out the contents of my handbag, examining everything—except the slim manuscript in the lining.

Once again I felt what I had felt before in Russia, most recently on my evening encounter with Solzhenitsyn when, without knowing why, I had started to run toward the Leningradskaya: the feeling of guilt in the absence of a sense of wrongdoing, of complicity in playing the other side of a shoddy, degrading game with the pale-haired official and his invisible masters. As I walked toward the Air-India plane, for a moment I had an intimate sense of what strength Alexander Solzhenitsyn must possess to play that game on an heroic scale, to dream of confronting Soviet authority not as victim but as an equal, even a superior power. And I felt a wave of fear at the—for him—

deadly venture ahead, whose success or failure now lay partly in my hands.

SEVERAL YEARS before that freezing Russian spring of 1967, an exceptionally courageous man, an admirer of Solzhenitsyn's literary talent, had brought out of the Soviet Union the microfilms of *The First Circle* in a pocket of his trenchcoat. For years he had kept them in a desk drawer in his study. Solzhenitsyn had asked him to have the book published only in the event of his death. Now, on a late April morning on my way back to America, I was visiting this man in his small apartment, which, filled with books and pictures, looked like a bit of Moscow tucked away in the middle of a great Western capital. As we smoked Gauloises and drank strong Italian coffee, which tasted wonderful after almost two months of the insipid brew that passes for coffee in the Soviet Union, I explained that Solzhenitsyn wanted me to take charge of publishing *The First Circle* in the West.

My host was silent. Sitting back in his armchair, he was attentively taking in what I had said. Then he got up and paced the tiny study where we had settled, puffing hard on his cigarette.

"He is a very brave man—but you, have *you* thought of his safety? Do you realize that your slightest miscalculation might kill him?"

My God, I had thought of nothing else since that night walk in Moscow. I tried to say this. Unconvinced, my host was describing in detail the danger that lay ahead for Solzhenitsyn if I did what he had asked. Sooner or later, as his decision to be heard outside of the USSR became known to the authorities, he could be shot from behind a corner by hooligans in the pay of the KGB. He could be killed in a car crash or simply be kidnapped and disappear forever. Why upset the present situation, which at least enabled him to go on with his writing? Was I certain I had understood him well? Was I not myself somewhat quixotic, carried away by my dream of building bridges that could not be built?

How easy it would have been at that moment to leave *The First Circle* in the hands of this man, intelligent and knowledgeable, who had at heart only Solzhenitsyn's safety and the survival of his literary work. His doubts echoed mine and made them loom larger. I tried to recall Solzhenitsyn's face as he had looked into mine in the pale glow of a Moscow streetlight, to make sure that I understood what it was that he was asking me to do.

"We must trust his instincts," I said. "He is a former *zek*, he has an intimate knowledge of the workings of the Soviet system. I think that he has an exceptional sense of survival sharpened by years in camp. He knows better than anyone the risk involved."

As we talked, I all the more longed for the moment when I could at last discuss the adventures of the recent days with my husband. I knew that the decision regarding Solzhenitsyn's request was for us both to make. Henry would bring to the project an understanding of practical realities. With some effort, I was now imagining *The First Circle* published in America, a thick novel that would have a red cover with gold lettering. This was the book about which its author had said: "A big book—my life." Now in English. For the first time I thought of its title in English and it sounded good. Would it be *The First Circle* or *In the First Circle*, I wondered.

At that moment, Solzhenitsyn's friend pulled out the drawer of his desk and took three small canisters of film from behind a pile of letters. He stood over me and dropped them in my lap one by one. He said, "Upon your responsibility." Then he added: "You can count on me. I will do everything in my power to help Alexander Issayevich and you in this project." This he was to do, unfailingly, in the years that followed.

I held the three film canisters in my hands. One was slightly rusted, containing perhaps a hundred feet of film. Another was small, made of spun aluminum. The third was plastic, black with a blue top. My host said: "As you can imagine, to bring these out safely was a challenge. Alexander Issayevich wanted me to carry them in a kind of money belt, a contraption which I was to wear under my shirt. A more conspiratorial, incriminating-looking object could hardly be imagined. Although Alexander Issayevich is a very stubborn man, I prevailed and carried the canisters in a pocket of my raincoat."

SPRING HAD NOT YET COME to the Northeast. At 5:00 P.M. it was cold as I stepped off the plane at Kennedy airport. Despite my fatigue, I was seized with an overwhelming feeling of relief as I approached the terminal building, already alight in the blue dusk. Any visitor returning from Russia experiences such a feeling; ironically, so did visitors in the prerevolutionary past. Going through the easy arrival formalities ("No fruits, vegetables, no foodstuffs, Cuban cigars . . ."), I thought of the cri de coeur of the Marquis de Custine upon his return to the West more than a hundred years before: "A bird escaped from its cage would be less joyous. I can speak. I can write what I think. I am free!"

Only this time I was not quite free.

MEETING HENRY OUTSIDE the customs area, hearing him ask about me, about the flight, the trip, I was more than ever aware of the chasm between my secure Connecticut life and the tortured world I had just left. How to bridge them? How was I to tell Henry of Solzhenitsyn's request? How, I kept wondering, would he react?

I remember driving up the parkways toward our home in northwestern Connecticut. I was safe. No one could arrest me. I could decide about what I had been asked to do. For, in returning to the West, I had now come to believe that Solzhenitsyn's commission presented us with a choice, to be deliberated and decided upon. Clearly I could not force my husband to drop his own work and devote himself to this enterprise, yet I needed his full-time participation if we were to proceed. If our decision was negative, we could delegate the responsibility to others, or let Solzhenitsyn know that he must find others to act for him. In the transition between Moscow and the dark, welcoming Connecticut hills, I had for the moment lost the feeling of mission that I experienced in Solzhenitsyn's presence, when he had searched my face to know whether I had fully understood what he was asking.

As we drove, I shared with my husband news of relatives and friends, passing on greetings of those, like Chukovsky and Nadezhda Mandelstam, who knew about him and thought of him as a friend. In turn, Henry gave me news of our son at boarding school, of his own work on his new novel, of our Connecticut and New York friends.

For an hour we caught up on everything—except the request which, despite my notion that we had freedom of choice in the matter, I sensed would have a momentous effect on our lives.

Why should we take on this task? From what I had learned in Moscow, I had no doubt that Solzhenitsyn would be able to find other people to act for him. I could not yet clearly imagine that the canisters of microfilm smuggled out of Russia and now in my possession, the manuscript of a book by an author not widely known in the West, would bring anything but disaster to him. The task he wished me to perform seemed as enormous as moving a mountain.

As clearly as I could, I told Henry of Solzhenitsyn's request. I stressed its urgency. Since I had all but given my assent on that walk to the Leningradskaya, I would have to inform Solzhenitsyn at once if we were to decline. If we were to proceed, it would mean setting aside all our own work. As I spoke I half hoped that when I had finished, my husband would say in a calm voice, "Olga dear, you must be still in Russia. We can't undertake a thing like that."

Henry said nothing of the sort. For years the plight of Russians threatened with a return to Stalinism had moved him too, and more than once he had asked in frustration, "How is it possible that in a country with a population of over two hundred million and a great literary tradition not *one* Russian novelist in fifty years has found the courage and vision to write the open truth about the Soviet Union?" As he listened now I sensed his excitement and it rekindled mine. Of course, he said, we had to do what Solzhenitsyn had asked. We could do it and do it well. It was—as I had felt in the dark street in Moscow only days before—an inviolable trust; it would be unthinkable to refuse it or to delegate it to others.

Even then, before either of us had read *The First Circle* or heard of *The Gulag Archipelago*, we realized, from what we knew of him and from *One Day*, that Solzhenitsyn's was the one Russian voice that had a chance to break the silence of the past half century.

For the rest of the drive and at home far into that night, Henry questioned me about every detail of my conversation with Solzhenitsyn. Reversing direction—for weeks I had been interpreting the West to Soviets—I told him everything I could remember about Solzhenitsyn and about the political climate in the USSR, with still vivid memories of urgent talks with friends in kitchens with the water running or the radio blasting; of the mute crowds filling the streets of Moscow with the soft, persistent scraping of their footsteps; and of my meetings with Solzhenitsyn.

We agreed that night that secrecy was the first and absolute priority. Quality of the translation and speed of securing its publication followed in importance. We would both set aside our own work and put all our energies to the task for a few months. It could all be done very quickly once we put our minds to it.

Rarely in a lifetime does one discover a purpose which, even in a minor way, transcends one's private world of family, friends, work, daily life, but such was our discovery then. It seemed that all our past, my Russian background and experience, Henry's seven years as an editor for New York book publishers, had been a preparation for the task of aiding Solzhenitsyn in the West.

At the same time, I still felt troubled. A childhood spent in emigration had taught me that Russian intellectuals are as a rule ill informed and uneasy about practical business matters. How, in fact, would Solzhenitsyn, formed by the Soviet outlook, regard our undertakings?

I did not share these thoughts with Henry. His positive response to Solzhenitsyn's request persuaded me that we should proceed.

From that first night, the mission to make certain that *The First Circle* would become an international literary event, and thus a protection rather than a threat to its author's life and freedom, occupied us totally, not for a few months but, along with the far greater responsibility later entrusted to us, for the next six years.

THE DAYS that followed were filled with what seemed one continuous conversation about Solzhenitsyn and *The First Circle*. Jet lag and fatigue dulled my senses, but my head was spinning Solzhenitsyn-related thoughts day and night. I felt that part of me was indeed still in Moscow.

All our attention was riveted on those film canisters and the man in Russia who had himself photographed the 500 pages of manuscript on as many frames of 35-mm film. Every sort of concern arose. How even to have the film printed without drawing attention? Was our copy of the manuscript complete and legible? Inspection showed severe fading on many frames. Were there, unknown to Solzhenitsyn, other copies of the manuscript in the West—a definite possibility since the KGB had "arrested" *The First Circle*? And most disquieting of all: Had my meetings with him been as secret as they had seemed?

Intuitively, I felt that we had not been noticed or recorded by the secret police in Moscow, but I could not rule out the possibility. Solzhenitsyn was under constant KGB surveillance, and the technology of electronic eavesdropping was so advanced that virtually no conversation within the USSR could be safely presumed to be confidential. Paranoia is not a Russian malady: In the Soviet Union, fears that one is being watched, followed, and may at any time be arrested are all too often justified.

But what about outside of Russia?

From the beginning we had to consider the possibility not only that my contact with Solzhenitsyn was known but also that

I could be used to build a case against him. This possibility was to haunt me for years.

In our redwood and glass house deep in a birch forest in rural Connecticut we immediately adopted modified Moscow rules for conversation. We knew that a telephone could be bugged to act as a microphone, which could then relay our conversation anywhere in the world, even with the receiver cradled. We began putting the telephone in the bread drawer or covering it with a big, soft cushion whenever we spoke of sensitive matters.

Looking back, I suppose that precautions such as these were overreactions, but, being unaccustomed to covert work of any kind and finding ourselves thrust into a situation uncomfortably similar to that of a James Bond scenario, by such measures we constantly reminded ourselves of extreme possibilities—and of the extreme consequences of a mistake.

In those first days, as spring began to be felt in the woods and the birches turned a lighter gray and bright green skunk cabbages were appearing among dead leaves, gradually, tentatively, I began to live again in the present, in New England instead of Moscow. But now the plight of Solzhenitsyn and all my Russian friends became even more anguishing to me, and vestiges of my Moscow experiences, more palpable than mere memories, made me doubt that this peace could ever again seem real to me. Closing my mind to all other considerations, I acted as a sort of medium, giving Henry as complete a picture as I could summon of what they faced in the Soviet Union.

By the first week I had read sections of *The First Circle* on the easel of a photographic enlarger and had impressions that the novel was indeed the long-awaited breakthrough in the portrayal of Soviet realities, a work of great literary and historical importance.

Our sense of urgency about proceeding safely with reproduction of the film, translation, and arrangements for publication became agonizing. How to begin—*safely?* We both had come to realize how little was explicit in Solzhenitsyn's directive, despite its military rhetoric, how much left to our judgment. Henry explained that in the area of publication, there were two distinct courses open to us. The first was to see the translation through (Solzhenitsyn had made it clear that I was to secure the translation) and then turn over the manuscript to a publisher without warranties, claims of authorization, or any further participation as Solzhenitsyn's intermediary. Let the publisher follow his own judgment, moral and commercial, as to what was best for Solzhenitsyn and his book. An obvious advantage of this procedure would be security against disclosure of my role and therefore Solzhenitsyn's. We could even leave the manuscript on the publisher's doorstep, anonymously, a very precious foundling.

The other plan was for me to act—secretly—for the author at every step of the way, guarantee to the publisher exclusive authorization and act as a link between author and publisher, taking decisions when communication was not possible and standing behind the publisher in defending the copyright.

Henry believed that the second plan, while more hazardous in the months before publication, offered the best chance for the novel to have the sort of success and worldwide attention that could bring its author fame and therefore a measure of protection. He knew that "big books" do not as a rule spring full-grown to become international bestsellers but are to a large extent the creatures of publishers who wager their resources on promoting those rare manuscripts they believe have the potential of achieving world acclaim. In other words, big books have to be both born *and* made. And no major publishing house is likely to venture capital and reputation, make the total commitment needed to create an international literary triumph, without the assurance that the author stands, even silently, behind it.

We had seen that the impact on non-Russian readers of Solzhenitsyn's *One Day* had been limited by the fact that the story, being first published in the USSR, could not obtain copyright protection under the then-existing conventions. The book was hurried into print by rival publishers watching each other over their shoulders, with none able even to imply a claim to authorized publication. Somehow, commercial incentives and quality of translation aside, the publication of a living author's text without his authorization, acknowledged or implied, is not likely to have the same effect as publication of the work with its author's assent even though it be secret. Not only is the uncorrected text itself suspect but a pall of questions also hangs over the unauthorized publication, as over that of a pseudonymous work. Is it truly the author's work as the author wished it to be seen? In 1963, when *One Day* appeared in the West, Solzhenitsyn had not been ready to engage openly in the combat in which his books were to be his armies. After its initial success he had retired to the privacy of his Ryazan existence, determinedly avoiding foreign journalists. Now, in 1967, he was ready for an international confrontation—with *The First Circle* committed on the front line.

The situation resembled in many ways that at the outset of world publication of *Dr. Zhivago*.

We had both followed the publication of Pasternak's novel, observing the vigorous defense of the copyright and the promotion of the book by the Milanese publisher Feltrinelli, who at every turn acted *as if* he possessed Pasternak's authorization, yet without openly claiming any arrangement with the author. In 1958, the novel was published with the success it merited. Here was the testament of a great poet brought to the world untainted by the Soviet state's degrading obsession to suppress truth in the USSR. Publication in each country was based on the presumption that an honorable compact existed between the Russian author and the Italian publisher, perhaps words exchanged one afternoon under the linden trees in the park at Peredelkino. Through an aura of legitimacy surrounding its publication, the novel escaped the stigma of being thought stolen from its author or disowned by him. Pasternak suffered deeply from the ostracism and vilification to which he was subjected in the Soviet Union, but his literary reputation remained untainted throughout the world.

In the years following the publication of *Dr. Zhivago*, a few Soviet books reaching the West threw scattered light on contemporary Russia. One, a novel by Ilya Ehrenburg, even lent its name to the optimistic era following Khrushchev's denunciation of Stalinism: *The Thaw*. But none shed any light on the vast darkness of the concentration camp universe. These books found readers in the West who gained fragmented glimpses into the fear-ridden Russia Stalin had left to the dazed survivors of his reign. One saw the gray lightening without seeing what it still concealed. People spoke of communism with a human face, seeing Khrushchev's face.

Then in 1962, with the publication in the Soviet Union of *One Day*, publication authorized by the First Secretary himself, light stabbed deep into the obscurity of decades, playing on the camps. Though only a narrow beam, it seemed an epochal event, one that must mean that fuller revelation of the world in which Ivan Denisovich scratched and plotted out his daily existence, the world of labor camps—indeed, of all Soviet life—would inevitably follow. It was not to be. Not then, not yet.

By 1967, most of us who visited Russia and followed Soviet affairs closely sensed that, on the contrary, the publication of *One Day* had marked an extreme swing of the pendulum in the direction of tolerance and that the return swing toward repression might already be underway. Yet the same lag in the recognition of present reality which permitted some of my Moscow acquaintances to believe that the thaw was an irreversible process that would necessarily end in a permanent cultural springtime in the USSR was also prevalent in liberal quarters in the West. One presumed—that bad as they still were, things were getting better. If what was whispered was true, they couldn't very well get worse. And in the United States, there were more urgent, focused calls upon attention and concern: Dallas, Saigon, Watts.

Indeed by 1967, officially at least, the author of *One Day* had faded into that tenacious obscurity from which he had briefly emerged. Solzhenitsyn had chosen to avoid attention and continue his work.

Pasternak, in *Dr. Zhivago*, had shown the West a Russia steeped in rich and tragic colors—a Russia that was gone. Now, with *The First Circle*, Solzhenitsyn was determined to show, in the starkest monochrome, the world that had taken its place, the Soviet Union behind the slogans and guard towers, seen through the eyes of a man whose vision and conscience were, by some miracle, not poisoned by what he had lived through. As Alexei Surkov was to observe, astutely, during the Writers Union confrontation with Solzhenitsyn on September 22, 1967, ". . . the works of Solzhenitsyn are more dangerous to us than those of Pasternak; Pasternak was a man divorced from life, while Solzhenitsyn, with his animated, militant, ideological temperament, is a man of principle."

An enemy to be destroyed.

By late May, I had read enough of the novel, projected on the enlarger easel, to be aware of its dimensions and quality—and the danger to its author if mishandled. The weight of my responsibility struck me with full force: there was no truly safe way to proceed. Yet proceed we must.

Believing that it would be Solzhenitsyn's wish, we chose the more hazardous path, the one we believed would lead to greater rewards: We would see *The First Circle* published, not furtively as another muffled outcry from the USSR, but as the masterpiece of world literature it is.

TWO

The Secret Circle

3

No safe way.

That visceral anguish one feels so often in Moscow, standing at a friend's door waiting for one's soft knock to be answered, not certain whether or not the visit is, for the friend, worth the risk— how strange to feel that anguish in our house in the Connecticut woods. Ordinary instincts begin to tumble. We had begun to live emotionally by Moscow rules.

Many times during the spring and summer of 1967 I inwardly resisted the plan to commit Solzhenitsyn's manuscript to large-scale publication in the West, fought against sealing my involvement as his representative, the guarantor that Solzhenitsyn himself stood silently behind the publication of *The First Circle.* Though we would of course verify with Solzhenitsyn, personally if possible, that precisely this plan in all its particulars was what he wished, questions would remain: How could he *not* deny all connection with his Western publishers should he ever be confronted by the Soviet authorities? How could the legal and commercial structure we were preparing *not* become a house of cards that would fall at the first breath? A fatal trap for Solzhenitsyn.

I was certain that a thunderous publication was what he wanted, knew that it offered the best chance to protect him. But a part of me longed for the less involving course, the safer one in the short run: to leave the manuscript on a publisher's desk and run; to leave decision to others. Would doing so have fulfilled Solzhenitsyn's trust in this "stern" woman in the picture in Chukovsky's study?

I knew it would not.

And indeed, once we had settled on the controlled-copyright, worldwide-publication plan, the path to its realization appeared with surprising clarity. What had once seemed to be merely accidents of our professional and personal lives now appeared as preparations for the job ahead.

Within a few miles of us lived two friends of ours who were also close friends of one another; each, in complementary ways, was qualified to aid us in the project. Both were experts, of long experience, in Soviet affairs; both were already keenly aware of the central role Solzhenitsyn was playing in the dissidents' struggle; both were persons of tested professionalism and unquestionable integrity.

Thomas Whitney and Harrison Salisbury.

Harrison had been head of the U.P.I. bureau in Moscow in 1944, had later spent five years in Russia as correspondent for the *New York Times,* which published the pioneering series "Russia Revisited" that in 1955 won a Pulitzer Prize. In 1967, Harrison was finishing his epic history of the siege of Leningrad, *The 900 Days,* He was also working on a special feature the *Times* was preparing on the occasion of the fiftieth anniversary of the Soviet Union. Aware that he had as much insight into Soviet affairs as any American, we knew he would prove to be an invaluable counselor. Through Harrison, we would be assured of receiving early information about Soviet affairs that might affect our decisions; at the same time, we would know that at least in one influential segment of the American press, the future clash between Soviet authorities and the defiant former *zek* in Ryazan would be reported with the benefit of accurate background. In every way, we were certain Solzhenitsyn would have in Harrison Salisbury a responsive friend in the West.

Tom Whitney, like Harrison, was a compassionate student of the Russian people under the Soviet regime. For years he had shared their hardships and perils as the husband of a Soviet woman, not allowed to leave the USSR with her until 1953. Tom's career included heading the economics section of the American Embassy in Moscow and a stint as the Associated Press's Moscow correspondent. In 1967, as now, he was a person whose enthusiasm for everything valuable and beautiful in Russia—her language, literature, art, music, and especially her people— amounted to a lifelong passion. At the same time, for all his appreciation of Russian art and life, he was, like his friend Harrison, a shrewd, unsentimental observer of the ever changing, never ending minuet of power in the Kremlin.

We looked to Tom Whitney for assistance on Solzhenitsyn's behalf in three areas: as translator of *The First Circle* (among his published translations was the most accurate version of *One Day*); as a second counselor whose combination of Russian expertise and hard American business sense would prove invaluable; and as the one in our inner circle who, if need be, could support the project financially, especially in its early stages.

At the time we decided to approach Tom Whitney we could not have had any idea of the magnitude of his future contributions to Solzhenitsyn's mission. We were still thinking in terms of a project that would occupy us all for a few months, a half year, and then end. I had always in mind the memory of Solzhenitsyn's exultant presence, the feeling of his grip on my arm, the memory of his asking me if I understood—the dark web of Moscow's bent streets, the weight of that watching night around us. Space had been transformed for me by that night, the weight of it was with me wherever I went; but time still had a terminus, a conclusion somewhere up ahead, whether welcoming or catastrophic I could not know. The project was all-absorbing but it would end someday and we would step away from it, proudly or in despair, depending on Solzhenitsyn's fate, but essentially as we had been before. It was not to end thus.

THE CHOICE OF PUBLISHER for *The First Circle* was also made during those first days after my return. To carry out a Zhivago-style publication effort we needed someone of great personal authority in a major publishing house, someone with whom we could deal confidentially, someone with the book sense to recognize, even before the translation was finished, that *The First Circle* was a literary work—and, potentially, a publishing event—of the first magnitude. We needed a publisher who would put Solzhenitsyn's safety before his own or his company's advantage, yet who on our signal would throw the full resources of a large firm behind the book and bring it out with resounding authority.

From among many able people he knew in the publishing industry, Henry proposed Cass Canfield, Sr., of Harper & Row as being personally qualified and professionally situated to do the best job with *The First Circle*. The fact that Cass Canfield was both friend and publisher of Harrison Salisbury was an added advantage, since it meant that he could obtain an opinion of the book, independent of ours, without further disclosure of its existence in the West.

Since Harrison and his wife were away at this time, I first phoned Tom Whitney, telling him we had something important to discuss. That afternoon he came to our house. We had put the telephone in the bread drawer. I remember that I was full of trepidation. What would Tom's reaction be to my encounter with Solzhenitsyn? Would he think that I was being too adventurous?

We sat down to tea. Henry told Tom about Solzhenitsyn's request. Tom was as fascinated and positive as Henry had been. There was no question, he told us; we must do what Solzhenitsyn wished. He said that he would help us in any way he could, agreeing to undertake the urgent job of translation.

Drinking cup after cup of strong tea as we would had we been in Moscow, we discussed the job ahead. It grew late, and the shadows of that May afternoon began to lengthen. In detail, we examined the means of preserving secrecy, the schedule of translation, the timing of publication, the probability of Solzhenitsyn's arrest and how we would then respond. As we talked, drawing upon Tom's counsel and his encouragement, we felt for the first time that camaraderie and dedication we would in the future find so supportive. Tom possesses sound New England virtues, including restraint—until his "Russian soul" takes over. Then this heavyset, white-maned American can be as enthusiastic as the wildest Muscovite.

So it happened that afternoon. Tom was with us. In Harrison Salisbury's absence, the next order of business was to see Cass Canfield.

THE DAY WE INVITED Cass Canfield to publish *The First Circle* remains in my mind as one filled with vivid correspondences and contrasts. Henry had arranged with Cass by phone that we meet, not at the Harper & Row offices, where we might be recognized, but at the Canfields' country house an hour southwest of us, near Bedford, New York. By coincidence, our friend Jill Fox, Mrs. Canfield's daughter by a former marriage, and her husband, Joe Fox, my editor at Random House, had invited us to a luncheon party on the same weekend we planned to see Cass, Sr. The Fox house adjoined Crowfields, the Canfields' estate. We were to go to the party and later leave unobtrusively and meet Cass.

Again I had the feeling that our steps were being guided, that the path before us was being opened by an unseen power, the branches in a magic forest parting as we approached the castle.

The day itself was an enchantment. On that brilliant May morning the first heat of spring had come to New England in an explosion of intoxicating sights and smells. We took back roads, past apple trees and dogwood in full bloom. After the nonstop conferences and concerns, I was pleased to be going to a party, out first outing since my return from Russia. I was also relieved to be taking the first decisive step.

We found the Foxes with some of their guests on the terrace. Others lounged in little groups on the lawn, enjoying the sun, looking out over a pond in the middle of which was a miniature island, forested enough to seem mysterious. There were guests strolling on the island; others stood near a newly built Chinese-style wooden bridge joining it to the freshly mown meadow. Farther down the grass a softball game was in progress. Others were up at the tennis courts, above the pond, in the direction of Crowfields. The sun was brilliant, spring was turning into a Breughel summer.

The talk on the terrace was witty and lively, New York literary gossip. We knew many of the guests. Among them were friends and associates of *The Paris Review*, the literary periodical that had staked my first trip to Russia in 1960 to interview Boris Pasternak.

All my life I had lived in and out of two, later three cultures, but I cannot remember a moment when I felt so torn apart as I did then by the incongruity between this carefree, amusing gathering, where serious and talented people were somehow able to play, to banter, to let life float pleasantly by on a lazy spring afternoon, and the tortured shadow-box world of my Moscow friends.

I was grateful when Philip Roth came over and asked me about my trip and about what was going on in the Soviet Union. From past conversations, I knew that Phil cared deeply for Russian literature. He was among the first of his generation to be concerned about the fate of intellectuals in Eastern Europe. It was possible for me to telegraph him that a new wave of reaction was engulfing Moscow. We discussed the trial of Yuri Daniel and Andrei Siniavsky, convicted of having had their works smuggled abroad for anonymous publication, and Solzhenitsyn, who, I said, was again emerging as Russia's leading literary dissenter.

As I spoke I wondered if Phil Roth, with his sensitive perceptions, could know that I was holding back something important. When one carries about a great secret, one crushes the instinct for candid talk with friends so violently that it seems the suppression must be obvious.

Had I read *Cancer Ward*? he asked.

Yes, I told him. I had been able to borrow the manuscript and had spent a sleepless night reading it in the Leningradskaya shortly before leaving Moscow. A remarkable book, strong, well constructed, full of feeling.

But there is another book, I wanted to add, an even more important book—important to Russian history—so dangerous to its author that . . . But I kept silent.

Phil asked me about what was happening at the Moscow Writers Conference, which was then in progress. Remembering Solzhenitsyn telling me of the "bomb" that would rock the muffled, self-serving assembly in May, I told him that I had no news but had heard in Moscow that there might be dramatic developments.

I wondered if the "bomb" had exploded yet. What would it be? Lillian Hellman had gone to the conference but had not yet come back. Through our channels we had as yet no news.

What dramatic developments? Phil asked.

I don't know, I told him. That, at least, was the truth.

We touched on other Russian matters, talked about Gogol, then Phil went off to join the softball game. I gazed out beyond the wooden bridge to the people talking in pairs on the island.

AT FOUR we left the party and drove up to the large manorial white house, with its white gravel circular drive and a broad view of unspoiled green hills dotted with apple trees. Nestled in the shrub borders, stylized animals greeted us—a deer, a swan, sculptures by Mrs. Canfield. As we got out of the car we could hear faint sounds of the party down the hill.

I remember a sudden, brief surge of panic. Here was the first move committing Solzhenitsyn and ourselves to the plan we had developed for *The First Circle*. It was not yet, of course, an irreversible step. Another trip to Russia would be necessary, we would have to present Solzhenitsyn with an entire organized program for him to accept, modify, or reject. Nonetheless we were about to test the interest of an American publisher in Solzhenitsyn as an emergent force in the world of letters. How were we to bring the spirit of my night walk with Solzhenitsyn into Crowfields? How could these worlds even touch, much less join in a secret project demanding total commitment and trust on both sides?

When the door opened and Cass himself stood there—tall, cordial, country-elegant, the very image of the Anglo-American gentleman publisher—I had a sinking feeling.

Jane Canfield came to greet us. We spoke briefly and very cordially—we had met the Canfields before, in San Francisco—then Cass excused us and ushered us into a small, pleasantly dark study off the main hall. With deliberate ceremony, he closed the door, seated us, sat at his desk. We were all quite close together and tense.

As Henry explained that what we were about to tell him must be kept absolutely secret, I watched Cass Canfield, thinking of what I knew about him. Of all the distinguished authors he had published in his long career, I could at that moment think only of Leon Trotsky—and just then the thought was not comforting. In that year, though he was nearing seventy, Cass looked much younger. He would suddenly shift his gaze and, with extreme intensity, settle all his attention on you. His long fleshy face was full of shrewdness; his blue eyes made you feel like a blossom in the path of a hummingbird. Gentleman he was and remained— even in the most trying and difficult times that followed—but I saw that his eyes were those of a hunter, a hunter of books now sensing a prize quarry nearby.

For I am sure that Cass did guess, even before we described *The First Circle*, perhaps had even gleaned it from Henry's brief phone conversation with him, that a publishing project of unusual importance was at hand. The best publishers know how to read people as well as manuscripts, and Cass was reading us now, intently.

Henry was telling Cass about the book Alexander Solzhenitsyn had given me the authority to offer for publication. I then told him all I could about it, its subject and dimensions, literary and historical importance.

Cass remembered *One Day* but had assumed its author had dropped back into obscurity, or suffered a worse fate. We explained that Solzhenitsyn had been hard at work, writing, gathering his forces, and was now about to confront Soviet authority in an attack in which *The First Circle* would be the main weapon.

Then Cass began to ask questions—and some of his questions alarmed us. Could he mention the project to one or two trusted colleagues? His lawyer? No, we said, definitely not at this time. But he could ask Harrison Salisbury to give an independent report on the novel. Cass must then decide whether he, on his own, wished to commit Harper & Row to an all-out publishing program. Others would be brought in only when absolutely necessary.

Would Solzhenitsyn openly authorize us to publish the novel?

Impossible, we told him; it would be, as in the case of *Dr. Zhivago*, a secret agreement with no public acknowledgment of the author's authorization or role in securing its publication in the West. Such disclosure would mean another sentence to a labor camp or even death.

How strange the words *labor camp* sounded in that house. I felt a million miles from the Plaza of the Three Railroad Stations. The delicately elegant furnishings in Cass's study suggested not the sharing of the desperate secret of a *zek* but the playing out of some lighthearted eighteenth-century intrigue.

Were there other manuscripts of the novel abroad?

To our knowledge, no, we told him, though the KGB had a copy. They might release it to spoil organized publication in the West, but only as a last resort, only if they were certain that such publication was forthcoming. We had heard about Victor

Louis, the high-living Soviet gadfly of the Novosti news agency and the KGB, who might at any moment offer a garbled manuscript of the novel to a minor Western publisher, then copyright it and lay a claim upon it. Victor Louis was yet another reason to keep the secret in the closest possible circle.

What about world rights?

Henry and I had discussed this question. Solzhenitsyn had simply asked me to publish *The First Circle*, saying that ours was the only manuscript he was releasing. Our assumption, which turned out to be correct, was that he meant publication throughout the world. Subject to the author's confirmation, we told Cass, world rights would be handled by Harper & Row. Seeing the look on Cass's face then, I spoke up to stress again that secrecy was our ruling consideration at this time and that all publication plans would be aborted if it were breached. We would be certain to cause Solzhenitsyn's downfall if a single word of our present conversation became public knowledge.

At a certain point during the next hour, as Henry and I responded to Cass's questions, I remember thinking that this visit seemed, after all, right: Cass's suppressed excitement, his intense concentration, and his questions, which in a short time showed us that he had become aware of the special nature and scope of the project, of the supreme daring of what Solzhenitsyn was undertaking, of what was at stake.

As we talked I remember trying in my imagination to bring Solzhenitsyn into the room with us. Would he approve the step we were taking? Would he sense Cass's professionalism, his nascent dedication to the project? Or would he, a Soviet, see only a Western businessman about to make a profit from a work steeped in Russian suffering?

Everything Solzhenitsyn had said about his book and its publication indicated that he wished to bring it to the world's attention not through the back alleys of Western publishing but through the main doors. He knew that my husband and I lived in the United States and that, in the absence of his instruction to the contrary *The First Circle* would initially be published there.

From the beginning I had been aware of an ambivalence in his thinking about the United States, a country he knew almost nothing about. During our evening encounter at the L.s', he had emphatically declared that America's material well-being had corroded the fiber of her people. Spirituality had disappeared from America because of excessive prosperity. I had protested. He had taken note of my protest without further comment, and I supposed that he had been speaking rhetorically, to test my reaction. Such a view of America was commonplace in the Soviet Union. But what if such was indeed his conviction? On the other hand, why would Solzhenitsyn turn to me and my American husband if he regarded the United States as the citadel of decadence and spiritual weakness in the West? Surely not on the strength of my Socialist forefathers, whose lack of practical sense he so keenly deplored.

By the time we left Crowfields the countryside was bathed in golden sunlight. Cass escorted us across the gravel drive to our car, assuring us that he would keep the secret and that he had the greatest interest in publishing Solzhenitsyn. We knew that we had found the right publisher for *The First Circle*.

And yet, when I tried to relate this moment to the other, only weeks before, to Solzhenitsyn searching my face in the dark street, I could not do so. The worlds were too distinct. Each obliterated the other.

Antiworlds.

All I knew was that for an unknown time I would be a voyager between them.

4

SHORTLY AFTER our visit to Crowfields, and in the company of Tom Whitney, we called on Harrison Salisbury at his farmhouse. In the small parlor where we talked, the New England spring morning flooded through the paned windows, beckoning us outside into the garden, where, in gloves and a broad straw hat, Harrison's wife, Charlotte, was tending her irises.

Harrison, tall and lean in country tweeds, could have passed for a mild-mannered, sixtyish professor on sabbatical. But, as we told him of my meeting with Solzhenitsyn, we were aware of the ardent newspaperman, adding this new information to his own broad knowledge of Soviet affairs. For he too was a hunter, tracking facts, leads, stories—stories of whole nations: Russia, North Vietnam, China. We knew him as a man of high integrity, with a professional journalist's concern to protect his sources of information. We trusted him. Nevertheless, when Henry began the story of my Moscow meeting and the collecting of the canisters, I glanced out the window at Charlotte, pretty and graceful in the rustic little garden sloping up to a green meadow, and for a moment I felt an almost irresistible urge to get up and walk out into the garden to join her, to cut short the conversation that had just begun—as if in revealing our secret, now for the third time, we were releasing forces we could never again control.

Harrison understood at once the idea of a publication directed by us on the author's instructions, with Harper & Row as holder of world copyright—it was indeed, he said, the best way of responding to Solzhenitsyn's request. He agreed to read *The First Circle* and tell Cass his opinion of it. We could count on him for this and for all the help he could give us. Excitedly we discussed Solzhenitsyn's strategies.

The following morning, June 5, the bomb Solzhenitsyn had mentioned to me in April would explode in the pages of the *New York Times*: a report on his letter to the congress of the Soviet Writers Union calling for an end to all censorship of Soviet literature and denouncing the Union for not defending its members from government harassment. Unfortunately, its detonation was to be somewhat muted in the louder explosion of real bombs— the opening battles of the 1967 Israeli-Egyptian war. But, perhaps thanks to Harrison, the item headlined SOVIET NOVELIST ASSAILS CENSORS, written by Theodore Shabad, was front-page news. To all of us, Solzhenitsyn's open letter, one part of the overall plan he had described to me, seemed to be further proof he was ready for battle. We had to carry out our assigned mission.

DURING THAT FIRST MEETING Harrison made a suggestion which was to be crucial to the project. It would also bring a new friend into our lives. If I was to act as Solzhenitsyn's representative, said Harrison, I would need a lawyer, both to assure that my relationship with Solzhenitsyn was established on solid legal grounds, and to ensure secrecy by acting for us in those negotiations in which our identities had to be kept secret. Moreover, large sums of money might be changing hands: we would need professional advice about managing these in Solzhenitsyn's best interest. Harrison recommended his own lawyer, who was also Tom's, a young man of proven ability and unlimited energy. His name was Anthony Curto.

I found the idea disturbing. Both Tom and Harrison we knew personally, Cass by well-established reputation and through his family. But Curto? Curto? To admit a stranger into our circle would be like leaving a protected harbor and entering the open sea. Did we really need a lawyer? Henry, with his practical sense and his familiarity with book contracts, had at first thought that in the interests of secrecy we would negotiate the contract ourselves and thereafter rely on Harper & Row's lawyers to defend Solzhenitsyn's copyright.

Now I saw that Henry was responsive to Harrison's advice. Tom agreed and spoke enthusiastically of Curto's competence and reliability. We did need a lawyer, and he was the right man. Everyone was making perfect "Western" sense, commercial and legal sense, but how to conciliate these with the spirit of my meeting in Moscow?

I thought of the man who had handed me the canisters. Would he approve? Would Solzhenitsyn?

Aware of my "Russian sensibilities," but firm nonetheless, Harrison repeated that we would after all be publishing the book under American law and customs, and, since it might stir worldwide interest and bring in considerable earnings, we had better be on sound footing from the start, to protect ourselves and Solzhenitsyn from entanglements that could give away the secret. Henry now agreed.

"You'll see," Harrison said to me. "Tony Curto will prove a great boost to your project. Don't let yourself be thrown off by his all-American exterior," he added. "You will find it useful to bring some solid common sense to your Russian adventure."

Before we left the Salisburys that morning, I too had agreed that we should meet with Mr. Curto. If we were to make this voyage at all it would have to be on the open sea.

TONY CURTO came to our house in Connecticut the following week, driving a big, most un-Russian Pontiac. It looked strangely oversized as he parked it in the dappled sunshine under our birch trees.

Tony, dressed in a dapper summer suit and tie, was a rounded, vigorous, pleasant-mannered, no-nonsense man in his early thirties. His easy smile sprang, I decided, from unassailable confidence in himself and the world he moved in. This world, I soon gathered, was one of private foundations, estate management, investments, shelters, mergers, trusts; a world, in short, so alien to the one I had left behind in Moscow as to aggravate my doubts that we were proceeding in the right direction. I suppose if I had imagined a lawyer for Solzhenitsyn's interests, it was an ascetic European intellectual, not this cheerful, pragmatic American, whose keen intelligence was steeped in the American success ethic, and who in the pleasantest possible way seemed to suspect everyone of the worst possible motives.

He apparently knew nothing about literature, little about the Soviet Union. He had had no experience dealing with women at a professional level, certainly he had never had anything to do with a Russian woman whose Slavic emotionalism was only partially tamed by a French education. But if I was an oddity to him, I had certainly never had anything to do with such an *American* American before. His air of exuberant well-being astonished me. So did his language, which combined imagery from Wall Street and Madison Avenue with legalisms—*fiduciary, disclosure,* and *specific performance*—which I found bizarre, threatening, and sometimes very funny.

Yet there was Tony in the big Eames-type chair in Henry's book-lined study. How does it all look to him? I wondered on that first day—the Russian classics mixed with American history on the shelves, the nineteenth-century Chinese desk and the worn Victorian rug we had inherited from Henry's grandfather on Nantucket? Everything about Tony was so new, from his shiny briefcase to his fresh shave and haircut. But he seemed oblivious of his surroundings. He was listening, questioning, giving every appearance of confidence that once he knew the facts, he could make his way in the new world we were introducing him to—not only make his way but lead us sure-footedly through whatever thickets lay ahead. At first I could not quite understand why from the beginning Henry listened—and made me listen—to legal considerations that seemed not only irrelevant to our mission but also often downright inappropriate. Why add *legal* problems to the *real* ones we already faced?

Early in our discussions, for example, Tony—who then had difficulty grasping the predicament of the Russian dissenters, much less the mentality of a *zek*—raised a question that seemed to me at the time proof of his insensitivity.

"Have you thought about *your protection*?" he asked it that first meeting.

Our protection! "Don't you understand?" I demanded. What mattered was not our protection but the protection of Solzhenitsyn's *life*, which was daily and nightly menaced.

"Yes, but to act for him as his fiduciary your own legal position must be secure. You can't help him if you're defendants in an action yourselves."

Fiduciary? Defendants? Action? Who would attack us?

"If the copyright were challenged, Harper & Row would have to defend it. You could be called to testify in court. If you refused . . ."

But Solzhenitsyn's life would be at stake!

"Then," pursued Tony, unruffled, "there is Solzhenitsyn himself."

Oh, I thought, the density of this man! He doesn't understand. He treats it as an ordinary business arrangement. Solzhenitsyn would *never* attack us.

"What if at some time in the future he was to be unhappy with the dispositions you made in his name? You have no executed agreement with him. You're vulnerable. There might be large sums of money involved. You could be liable."

And so on. I was making a great effort to decipher Tony's language. It would be quite some time before I realized that each battling sentence he uttered that June day referred to situations that might indeed occur.

As Tony ranged over the possible problems he not only fanned smoldering doubts I already had, he ignited new ones as well. Besides financial and legal liabilities, he spoke of possible impairment of our professional reputations. He raised possibilities that seemed both frightening and beside the point. I began to feel, in those peaceful Connecticut woods, the same Kafka-like guilt in the absence of crime that I had felt in Moscow. Perhaps my artist's instincts were right after all: avoid entanglements and business commitments. Stay free. Read books. Look at pictures. Travel. Pursue your own work. How against the grain this involvement seemed then, bristling with more risks than I had ever imagined. Yet Henry remained undisturbed, certain that it was the right way. I steeled myself by remembering my exchange with Solzhenitsyn about the Socialist Revolutionaries, their inability to act. Surely he did not want an SR do-nothing approach to *The First Circle*.

At that first meeting a relationship developed between the three of us which was to set a pattern for all our future dealings. I spoke from the point of view of Solzhenitsyn and others in Moscow, Tony from that of a lawyer weighing the consequences of our projected actions, Henry as a strategist leading us toward decision and also as a moderator of the differences that arose between Tony and me, interpreting one to the other, sometimes siding with me, sometimes with Tony—and sometimes getting caught in sharp crossfire between us.

That late spring and early summer, the three of us met often, in Connecticut and in Tony's midtown Manhattan office. I remember particularly the morning sessions in the country. Tony would arrive early. I would scurry around for a robe that was neither a negligee nor sloppy, plug in the electric coffee maker and bring mugs of hot coffee into Henry's study, where we would talk—away from the telephone. Tony would sit in the big chair, Henry at his Chinese desk, I on the floor on a cushion.

After the first few encounters, Tony got used to my Russian ways and quickly came to share our sense of mission. For my part, I began to see that what I had at first taken for a lawyer's obsession to complicate matters with legal niceties was in fact a concern to make sure that the project would stand up to any future test.

Still Tony and I clashed often.

He was learning from me about the isolated world of Russian dissenters, about book publishing from Henry, while instructing us both in the law. My education in the law of copyright, contracts, and trusts proceeded rapidly—and always, at each step toward the commitment of the novel to publication in the West, I asked myself obsessively how Solzhenitsyn would regard all this. Aware of his lack of knowledge of the West, I wondered how he could possibly understand, as I was beginning to, the need for the elaborate legal and commercial structures we were developing.

Both Tony and Henry thought my fears excessive. Solzhenitsyn's request, they said, was clear, his trust in me implicit. With respect to *The First Circle*, I was, under Western law, its author's trustee, and as such had legal responsibilities. The publisher would expect certain warranties. Again and again we discussed the question of keeping our role secret. Under what circumstances could we be forced to answer questions in a court of law? I said that I would go to jail before I would breathe a word of my relationship to anyone, law or no law. But how could we ensure secrecy at Harper & Row?

Were we not leading Solzhenitsyn to disaster?

I knew that the course we were taking made sense—but only Western sense. From the Soviet viewpoint we were deliberately and unlawfully committing a manuscript written by a member of the Writers Union to the mainstream of capitalism. Large advances against royalties—viewed by Henry as the best way to ensure a large-scale publishing effort with maximum publicity and attention—were to be received on Solzhenitsyn's account. The case against him in Russia, were the secret to leak, would be devastating. But if the secret were kept, our strategy would be likely to strengthen his position in Russia once publication took place. Everything depended on secrecy.

The worst part of it for me was that at that time only I, as a frequent visitor to the USSR, was aware that *whatever he might say or do* Solzhenitsyn himself, educated in the same system of values as those of his enemies in the Soviet establishment, must to some degree share that deeply conditioned suspicion of the West, of capitalism, of the profit motive within free enterprise.

There was no reason for Tony to understand that Solzhenitsyn might feel ambivalent about his decision. If Henry shared my concern, he did not let it slow our work toward publication. We had faith that the book's success—carrying with it the worldwide recognition of Solzhenitsyn—would orbit *The First Circle* above the political arena and strengthen his defense against arrest and destruction, and it was on that faith that we based our plans.

All this planning absorbed enormous amounts of time and energy, although as far as most of our friends were concerned we appeared to be leading the same life as before, writing our books, giving and going to informal country dinners, spending a few days at Henry's family house on Nantucket. But on the inside the texture of our life was altered. Our fifteen-year-old son, Michael, at home from school for the summer and aware of our secret, thought we had lost all sense of measure. Did we have to be quite so single-minded, so intense about Solzhenitsyn? He was intrigued with our new involvement and fully understood its confidentiality—but why the endless discussions? Why the tensions? Yet at all times we had to be alert for news and messages from Russia, on guard against somehow revealing the secret, anxious that we or others might be careless, that is to say, human. No longer could I write what I felt in my articles about the Soviet Union, for fear of bringing myself to the attention of Soviet authorities. No longer were our lives our own. The feeling that we were a small but crucial part of Solzhenitsyn's mission was both exhilarating and disturbing, and though the new secret side of our lives was obviously necessary, I was never to get used to it. I think it was easier for Henry—discretion and restraint were part of his upbringing.

In June of 1968, the films were printed in two copies of 504 large slippery white pages, Tony personally supervising the entire operation to be certain that no extra page was out of our hands. Tom Whitney was soon hard at work on the translation. Harrison had left for Russia, where he was to stay until August working on the Soviet anniversary project for the *New York Times*. On June 22 a story in the *Times* reported that the Writers Union was to see to the return of Solzhenitsyn's confiscated manuscripts, approve publication of a suppressed short story, and let him travel abroad. These were false promises, made by the Soviet government in an effort to appease Western public opinion on the eve of the anniversary.

On June 24 we had a second encounter with Cass Canfield. We met for lunch at a restaurant near Bedford. Time and reflection had whetted his interest in publishing Solzhenitsyn. Harrison had already reported to him that *The First Circle* was indeed of the very greatest historical and literary importance. So we met less to convince him of the novel's importance than to discuss plans and tactics. We considered the need of a forthcoming trip to confirm our arrangements with Solzhenitsyn, and Cass offered financial assistance, which I declined, resolving not to incur any obligation to a publisher until I had secured Solzhenitsyn's approval of our plan. I was fascinated—and made uneasy—by Cass's account of his publishing that other Russian author of his, Leon Trotsky. Cass's stories were in striking contrast to the atmosphere of the country inn. Its leafy terrace and checked tablecloths evoked the Impressionists. But then Cass had surely entertained Trotsky also at carefree festive meals—until the Bolshevik leader's ugly death in Mexico.

We parted with renewed pledges of secrecy.

On July 14, Harrison reported in the *Times* that Solzhenitsyn's "arrested" manuscripts were being returned to him and that the ban on publishing one of his novels, *Cancer Ward*, was being lifted. He also reported that favorable reaction to Solzhenitsyn's May letter calling for the abolition of censorship had led many Soviet writers and other intellectuals to believe that censorship was in fact about to end. From my own recent impressions of Moscow, I could only wonder, with some skepticism, whether the now famous May bomb would in fact produce such a change.

Then in July, we received word from Solzhenitsyn: He wanted *The First Circle* published in the winter of 1968. We had known since my meeting with him that the novel was to be published without delay. Now, with the job of translation only begun, and, knowing the time needed by the publisher to produce a book once a manuscript has been delivered, we would have to act at breakneck speed if we were to meet the new deadline. And there would have to be another meeting with Solzhenitsyn, at which all our plans would be presented for his approval or rejection.

But how was I to arrange the trip without running too great a risk of compromising him? Henry had insisted all along that we act *as if* there was someone in the USSR putting together all the pieces of the puzzle in which we were involved, waiting for one more to complete the picture and crush Solzhenitsyn. There had to be a KGB agent exclusively assigned to investigate Solzhenitsyn's foreign relationships, so that the authorities could pounce whenever they felt the time had come to destroy him as a dangerous foe of the State. According to Henry, in all likelihood, it was only a question of time.

That summer, as in a dream, the night streets of Moscow were drawing me back, at once forbidding and irresistible. My wintery April in Moscow seemed far more compelling and real than the seemingly endless, serene New England summer.

THREE

Return to Moscow

5

ARRANGEMENTS FOR MY TRIP fell into place easily. I had another reason to be in the Soviet Union that fall. For a long time my friend and neighbor Ingeborg Morath Miller and I had been collaborating on a picture book about Pasternak's world; she was to take the photographs while I would write the text. That summer, Arthur and Inge Miller decided to tour extensively in the USSR, and they invited me to join them for part of their trip. For me, this meant an opportunity to work on our book and to travel, under the best conditions, to places other than Moscow and Leningrad and in the company of the most stimulating of friends. I in turn could provide them with introductions to Russian acquaintances who were difficult to contact, among them Nadezhda Mandelstam and Joseph Brodsky.

The trip also provided the needed opportunity to meet with

Solzhenitsyn, without—I hoped—any interested authorities wondering why I was so soon again in Russia.

Because at the last minute Arthur had been delayed by his work, Inge and I set off alone. Arthur would catch up with us later. It was September and the two of us delighted in the mild Indian summer days in northern Russia, strolling under the sun-flaked white walls of Novgorod, roaming the fields and forests of Pushkin's estate near Pskov. We sustained ourselves with apples and caviar and together made new Russian friends. Then we flew south for a few days in Soviet Georgia, and it was there that Arthur met us.

I fell in love with Georgia, a lyrical, hospitable place of landscapes in which the grandiose and the human meet in majestic, patriarchal harmony. In all, I traveled twelve days with the Millers. They would have been blissful were it not for the nagging anxiety that my grasp of all the detailed planning we had done in the United States, of all the complex proposals and questions concerning the worldwide publication of *The First Circle* that I would soon have to present to Solzhenitsyn, in the space of a few minutes, might vanish in the blue-gray smoke of festive Georgian cooking fires, in the haunting music of accordions and drums. Still, such was the power of Georgian poetry, which sounded to me both exotic and wonderfully familiar, that it assuaged these anxieties.

Another, deeper fear would not pass. Somehow I already sensed that this visit to Russia would be my last for many years, perhaps forever. I began to experience everything as if this were so. In the studio of David Kakabadze, who had studied in Paris, we looked at the painter's own whimsical abstractions and at his collection of huge canvases by Nico Pirosmani, the great Georgian primitive. Both men in their lifetimes had had difficulties with the established order, yet in that studio I felt as if both artists were still alive and as if Georgian art continued to flourish unmolested; I thought of the cruelty of political separations, of people caged all their lives in their homelands, others barred from them in perpetual exile.

I remember saying good-bye to the exuberant young theatrical director who had escorted us there. We said *Do svedanya* as if we would really see him again, and he replied with the same certainty: "Until we meet again." Then he gave me a slim blue volume of Georgian poems in translations by Pasternak and Akhmatova, saying: "Let's open it to a chance poem, it will tell us about our next encounter." The book fell open to lines by Tabidze; addressed to Balmont, a Russian poet who was to die in emigration in Paris, they spoke of impossible reunions:

> *Now we wait for you along the road of friendship,*
> *And again, like brothers we greet you among us*
> *And raise the pale blue drinking horns in your honor.*

From Tiflis I flew back to Moscow. The Millers went on to Samarkand. I had been careful not to involve them in anything having to do with Solzhenitsyn, yet I felt uneasy about keeping the secret from these close friends. I knew that it was necessary, but I hated it.

I arrived in the capital on a late September morning, the Indian summer lingering and Moscow iridescent and blue as if lighted from within, exactly as I had wanted to see it in the spring. Not without regrets I decided to limit my encounters to people who were sufficiently well established not to have much to fear from their association with me if my connection with Solzhenitsyn were ever to come to light. I would spend most of my time with my favorite older friends, Nadezhda Mandelstam and, especially, Kornei Ivanovich Chukovsky. They were the people whom I might indeed not see again in this world, those from whom I had most to learn both about the past and my own place in the present.

Kornei Chukovsky was then in his mid-eighties. He had once been my grandfather's friend, he was now Solzhenitsyn's—indeed, it was presumably through him that the author of *One Day* had learned about me.

Did Chukovsky know of Solzhenitsyn's request to me? I expected that he did not. I hoped that he did not, yet in another way, I wished he did—his approval of such an undertaking would have meant everything to me.

Tall, snowy-haired, vigorous, his face ruddy and full after a "good summer's work" as he put it, Chukovsky received me that September in his ample wooden *dacha* at Peredelkino, the writers colony southwest of Moscow where, in 1960, I had often come to visit him and Pasternak. Chukovsky greeted me with particular warmth, as if he too sensed that this autumn's encounter might be our last. As on my earlier visits, he soon turned the conversation to Andreyev, whom he had loved and had admired for his talent, considering himself his protegé. This time too he played the game he had played with me ever since my first visit. Each time, he would try to pay me back a hundred rubles he said Andreyev had lent him in his impecunious youth. I would refuse. Chukovsky would persist, distracting me with wonderful anecdotes about my grandfather—how he had once lain down between railroad tracks and let a train pass over him, how he had received guests in his spectacular wooden mansion in Finland, where my father had grown up, how after my grandmother's death the elegant ladies of Petersburg had literally lined up to meet him—while all the time trying to tuck a hundred-ruble banknote into my pocket or my purse.

Over tea with black bread and butter, he told me about Andreyev's and Gorki's stand against anti-Semitism in an era of government-promoted pogroms. And about Andreyev's love for my grandmother, known as Lady Shura, a delicate woman of great inner strength who had helped my grandfather overcome his drinking problem. She had also been an inspired literary critic. "She died in childbirth—her death so young was a tragedy for Andreyev and for Russian literature."

After his afternoon nap, a ritual he regarded as essential to his continued literary proficiency, Chukovsky took me for a walk along the narrow lanes of Peredelkino, still summerlike and fragrant in the late September sun. He told me about the dissident movement, lowering his booming voice as we strolled under the firs along the lanes. Ardently he talked about the dissenters he knew and admired most—Andrei Sakharov, the Litvinov family. To one who had kept silent, at least in public, all through the Stalin years, the boldness of these independent voices was a revelation and an inspiration. I gathered from what he said that now he was helping others besides Alexander Solzhenitsyn.

When he mentioned Solzhenitsyn's name there was nothing in his voice to tell me whether he knew of my spring meetings with the writer. All I could be certain of was that his own assistance to Solzhenitsyn and others, while secret, had given him a new taste for life. He held his handsome head high and his movements, always energetic, had a new dramatic assertiveness. Once the soul of prudence, he now voiced his disgust with the KGB and the turn Soviet politics was taking, giving emphasis to his feelings by waving his arms as we walked and sometimes clapping his fist loudly into the wide open palm of his hand.

I wondered how much his recent houseguest had inspired Chukovsky's new outspokenness. Certainly there was intense joy in his breaking free from a half century of enforced silence.

I paid several visits to Chukovsky that fall. Sometimes I would stay overnight in a small downstairs bedroom of the wooden house. Though this was against Intourist regulations, we counted on his great popular reputation and lifelong friendship with my family to excuse the infraction, should I ever be questioned. Always on these occasions we took evening walks down the lanes of the colony, past dimly lit cottages half hidden behind tall lattice fences with ornamental tops. Each stroll was a little different. He would point out certain houses, naming their occupants, past and present—Babel, Pasternak, Katayev, and the literary powers of the Soviet establishment, Fadeyev and Tikhonov—and would tell stories about them, darting back and forth in time, until the breach between past and present began to close as Chukovsky shared his eighty years of memories with me. Sometimes we would pass other strollers and he would exchange a word, then when we had gone a safe distance tell me who it was, in the most candid, sometimes unflattering terms. Once I remember passing a man with a face that reminded me of a wolf's. Chukovsky spoke to him, without introducing me; then the man turned into the gateway of a house my guide had already identified. It was Konstantin Fedin, the head of the Writers Union, who was to become Solzhenitsyn's archenemy in the months to come.

I always slept well at Chukovsky's. I loved the pinewood smell of the room, the narrow bed with its old-fashioned quilt; I felt at home in this wooden house creaking with presences—Chukovsky; his elusive daughter Lydia, herself a marvelous writer; his secretary, Clara, ebullient, feminine; the elderly housekeeper with her wrinkled peasant face—each having a life that followed laws of its own. Away from the Soviet hotel with its stony-faced surveillants on every floor, I felt protected by the tall trees around the *dacha* and warmed by the images of Andreyev and Lady Shura which Chukovsky had drawn for me.

Better than anyone else in Russia, he knew how to create a sense of life's continuity for one brought up in the limbo of emigration. One afternoon, on an earlier visit, he had had a special surprise for me, one that joined past and present in a way I would never forget. He had called me out into the garden, where a drab gray truck, like a closed delivery van, was parked under the trees. Two young men stood by the truck. With the authority of a theatrical director, Chukovsky set them in motion. One opened the back of the truck and I saw that it was filled with electronic recording equipment. It was a sound truck from a Moscow TV station, which was making a filmed interview with my host. Chukovsky climbed inside. Both young men disappeared after him. Soon Chukovsky summoned me into the crowded interior and handed me a pair of earphones. I put them on and heard a lot of crackling, some coughing and wheezing noises, then a male voice, strangely enthusiastic, slightly breathless. It resembled my brother's voice. It was youthful, aware of its own effect, a bit tentative because of this. I realized that the man speaking was my grandfather. He was addressing a political rally more than half a century ago; he would have been about my age then, or younger. When the recording ended I took off the earphones with wonder. Chukovsky was nodding in delight.

"This is the live Andreyev—Andreyev's live voice," he assured me.

Days before my scheduled arrival, he had arranged to have the recording machinery brought to his house. Chukovsky was the closest thing to a magician that one could hope to meet in this life.

Now again in Peredelkino I thought back to that day: What would the "live Andreyev," who loved Russia passionately, have thought of Solzhenitsyn's stand? And of my own participation in his mission? Might the fact that it was covert cause him to disapprove? Or would he feel that to fight bolshevism through literature was legitimate? That day, despite Chukovsky's friendship, I remember feeling very lonely.

On these visits in 1967 Chukovsky spoke more and more about Solzhenitsyn and still I could not tell how much, if anything, he knew or guessed about my acquaintance with the writer. I learned only that Solzhenitsyn had in fact inquired pointedly about me while studying the "stern" photograph. From long habit formed during the Stalin era—despite his new candor—Chukovsky was careful not to discuss other people's affairs, which if known might prove dangerous to them and to himself. In 1960, he had deliberately made it extremely easy for me to meet Boris Pasternak while ostensibly discouraging me, with vigorous waving of arms and stamping of feet, from ever trying to call on him. Now he spoke with enthusiasm about Alexander Solzhenitsyn while at the same time cautioning me about "this man who is possessed" (*oderzhimiy*), for all his restrained, even affable exterior. He was the first to suggest to me that Solzhenitsyn's experiences in camp had made him into a very complex, steely human being.

These were passing remarks, dropped in the course of the warmest praise for Solzhenitsyn. And I was, in any case, determined to discount them, just as seven years before I had ignored Chukovsky's injunctions not to visit Pasternak.

He praised Solzhenitsyn for his literary achievements, the richness of his idiom, his courage. A hard-working, highly organized writer himself, Chukovsky appreciated Solzhenitsyn's ability to concentrate, the speed with which he wrote. The speed, especially, he found phenomenal.

"His scientific formation and his camp background aren't enough to explain it," he told me, a professional giving full credit to another professional's technical mastery. "While he was staying here, during the midnight Easter mass at our little church, hooligans started hounding the crowd which had gathered to attend the service. An ugly incident. He wrote a story about it. Did it in one day. Just sat down and wrote it."

Chukovsky was worried about Solzhenitsyn's survival. He had witnessed local toughs in the pay of the police trying to intimidate the author of *One Day*. Avoiding detail, he hinted at calamity ahead.

"It's worse when he's home in Ryazan. At least here I'm 'Grandfather Kornei.' Has some effect on these scoundrels. There—*chort!* All hell breaks loose! *Chort, chort!*"

And once again, as he spoke, he seemed to sense that these would very likely be my last visits with him. "You with your literary friendships in the West, you ought to alert international opinion to this damnable situation. Russia's most promising writer hounded by riffraff! Dreadful! Do you realize that the man is nearly destitute? And fiercely proud—won't accept a thing from anyone."

Then with hardly a pause he added, "Funds must be raised. Money to help him. Why don't you do something about it when you get back to the United States?"

When I inquired how funds could reach him if he refused all material aid, Chukovsky waved this question away. Somehow funds had to be raised *and* a way found to make them acceptable to Solzhenitsyn. He would take it upon himself to induce him.

Chukovsky must have brooded on the question, because later in the day he took it up with his beloved talking lion. This was a present someone had sent him from America. It was an oversized, bright yellow stuffed animal, a standing lion with a smiling face and a stubby tail. Whenever the tail was pulled the lion spoke in a very deep voice, with what sounded like a New York accent.

"I am the Cowardly Lion," the animal would say. This was followed by a couple of unintelligible sentences, which Chukovsky chose to interpret at will—his lion was his oracle.

Making a face at the lion, he turned his attention to me, saying, "On the other hand, Olytchka, now that I think of it—and my lion agrees with me—it's not at all a good idea for you to concern yourself with Solzhenitsyn's affairs. You shouldn't compromise yourself and your family. The more I think about it, the more I think you should remain a free observer. Let those of us who live here take this sort of responsibility. Yes—that is what the lion says, do you hear him?" he added, pulling the lion's tail. "And now let me tell you about your grandfather's house. You should have seen the huge tile stoves, the rugs, the massive Scandinavian furniture. The most beautiful women in Petersburg would arrive in horse-drawn sleds, bundled in furs. . . ."

I sat perplexed. Had Chukovsky merely been recanting his own suggestion about aiding Solzhenitsyn, or was he referring to my secret engagement with him—and warning me to abandon it? I could not tell. Now, like a prestidigitator, he drew living pictures of the house in Finland, the guests entering its spacious main hall, the fireplaces, the white bearskin rugs, Andreyev appearing on the stairs in a black velvet jacket, lost in sorrow, grieving for his lost Lenore, Lady Shura, and, Chukovsky told me, for Russia, whose future he saw as dark and frightening.

Yet his words of warning worked deeper than these images. In a soft voice he quoted Alexander Blok:

> Children, if you could only know
> Of the cold and fear of future days.

I was never to discover what Chukovsky knew about my relationship with Solzhenitsyn. Whether or not he was aware of it, his warning impressed me deeply. It seemed to echo my own innermost voice. And yet it was necessary that I disregard that warning.

6

A FEW DAYS LATER, by arrangement, I saw Solzhenitsyn. We met one evening at the home of yet another set of acquaintances. He had grown a beard. His face had lost some of its sharpness. The signs of extreme inner tension I had observed that spring seemed gone. With his short reddish beard, he now looked like a Russian warrior. As he glanced at me across the table where we sat over tea, he seemed confident, in control of his powers, almost exultant, a guerrilla commander on the eve of a major engagement.

There was general talk for a while about politics, Soviet and American, then Solzhenitsyn got up, indicating that I should follow him. This seemed to astonish no one. These were all trusted friends. He led me out onto a narrow, partly enclosed balcony, like a cave opening. It was a cool, pleasant night. Below, streetlights, blurred by mist, curved away from us through a still, anonymous cityscape. I remember a faint smell of decaying leaves, the necklace of streetlights, and feeling certain then—I was not to be so sure later—that in this isolated spot we could not be spied on or overheard.

Despite that certainty, I was more tense than ever before in my life. All summer I had prepared myself for this moment. Henry and I had developed analogies for breaking down complex legal and commercial issues, so that Solzhenitsyn could understand at once the structure that his urgent words to me that spring were now creating in the West. In all my years of living in and out of different cultural worlds, of doing my best to interpret one to another, I had never before had to build such a fine-spun bridge on which so much depended. I felt like Marco Polo about to be received by Kublai Khan for five minutes to explain the laws of Venice.

Worst of all, though my mind was clear about what I had to tell him, I was keenly aware of Solzhenitsyn's own exhilaration, his desire to communicate to me, on a different plane, his great new decisions, his schemes, his mission. The faint glow of the sky above us reminded me that we were in Moscow, where both St. Basil and the Lubyanka stand. What appeared reasonable and desirable in Connecticut might here appear meretricious and dangerous, if not lunatic.

Could Alexander Solzhenitsyn be bound to contracts and trusts?

At that moment we were two Russians on a narrow balcony, I with a strange message from another planet. Antiworlds.

I took a breath and began.

"Alexander Issayevich, what has been done so far is this. . . ."

At first, all my fears seemed justified. As I began to outline the legal arrangements we proposed for controlled publication of *The First Circle*, Solzhenitsyn seemed hardly to hear me, interrupting with extraneous comments. When I spoke of the contract to be drawn with Harper & Row, of simultaneous publication in all countries, world rights, copyright, Solzhenitsyn seized upon the word *simultaneous* and spoke heatedly, exuberantly, of salvos and crossfire. He told me that he had now determined to be the victor in his duel with the KGB that had been going on for months. The publication of *The First Circle* abroad was essential to the success of this battle. His voice shook as he spoke of the KGB. How he hated the scum! After "arresting" his novel, one he had had no intention of disseminating—at the time of the seizure he had not shown *The First Circle* even to his closest friends—the KGB was devising ever new methods to crush him, to discredit him throughout the Soviet Union, to demoralize him, his family, his friends. Now he would retaliate in a way that the authorities could not envision in their wildest dreams.

"Yes," I said, "and to accomplish that . . ."

"Yes!" he interrupted. "*The First Circle* must appear as a complete surprise, a bombshell!"

And he went on, scarcely letting me respond: Money for the project could be had from Fawcett, an American paperback publisher who was holding for him some royalties from *One Day*. Money must be spent freely, nothing must be spared. There must be no thought to money.

Desperation must have entered my voice as I explained—aware of time racing by with so much still to say—that it would be a needless risk to open the secret to any other publisher. Funds would be advanced by Harper & Row as soon as I returned with his approval of the plan I was submitting to him. Harper & Row would control world rights under a contract secretly signed by me as his trustee. Expenses would be paid and the balance held for his disposition. There was no difficulty about this. Through a trust, it all could be managed with minimum risk. No document with his signature was needed.

Yes, but we were to spend money to advance the project freely, as if it were our own. He laid great stress on this.

Precious minutes were passing. My planned presentation seemed to be breaking up like waves against a rock. I had the impression that Solzhenitsyn was regarding the moment not only as a meeting to exchange information and conclude plans, but also as a ceremony to confirm in grand terms, insofar as *The First Circle* was concerned, that his powers and directives were to flow, at his sole bidding, through me.

On the balcony I had my first glimpse of Solzhenitsyn the autocrat.

I was not reaching him. Or so I despairingly thought. Yet almost in the same instant, I saw Solzhenitsyn, the supremely intelligent strategist, more responsive to what I was telling him than I had at first perceived.

Our eyes accustomed to the darkness, each of us could now see the other's face by the faint lights of the city. He must have read my distress and sensed what caused it. Again, as he had done on our walk, he took my arm and held it firmly. Yes, he told me, financing through Harper & Row was indeed the safer and better way. Secrecy was more important than ever now—one careless word, one false step and he was dead. Yes, he understood that in the United States we had gathered a small circle of trusted friends, each making his contribution; that the translation was under way; that Harper & Row stood ready to publish *The First Circle* in 1968. It must be at Christmas, he told me; the bomb must explode on exactly the twentieth anniversary of the events described in the story. The work must progress at full speed. In secrecy, but there was no time to lose. Not a day.

I was relieved, yet there was still so much to say, so much to ask. We were both aware that there was little time left during which we might talk. Our absence from the gathering inside was already lasting too long.

Headlong I went over the point most difficult to project: the importance of a strong, invisible chain of legal authority leading secretly from him through me to Harper & Row and then openly through them to every other publisher of the novel throughout the world. The chain must hold fast, for if it broke we could face piracy, conflicting claims by publishers, disruption of publication by Soviet agents, exploitation of the novel as deliberately anti-Soviet, and, worst of all, the risk of disclosure of our relationship —something that could mean real danger for Solzhenitsyn. If the chain broke, we would find ourselves with an explosive cause célèbre on our hands instead of a manuscript to be brought to light as a major work of literature.

To prevent this from happening, we needed his confirmation of my exclusive power to act for him in everything concerning publication of *The First Circle*. We also needed his assurances that he would not release other copies of the manuscript in or out of Russia for months to come. We needed his approval of the method of publication. I also told him that if his safety necessitated it, he could publicly denounce the publication, just so long as he assured us, through channels and codes already developed, that in fact the invisible chain of authorization held fast.

My heart was pounding now. Had he understood? Had I made myself clear? Was this what he wished?

"Yes, Olga Vadimovna, that is exactly what I wish you to do," he said solemnly. "I have the feeling that a higher destiny will bring success to this undertaking. I feel that you have understood its spirit."

When I think back to that moment ten years ago, I am certain that prior to this encounter Solzhenitsyn had developed detailed plans of his own, procedures, such as my going to the paperback publisher for funds, which he intended to tell me to act upon. On learning that we had already devised a plan, one that awaited only his word to be set in motion, he may not have been pleased. But as he reflected on what I had just said, I saw him begin to relax and smile, as if he understood then that the publication of *The First Circle* was much nearer realization than he had imagined, and that it would be carried out in a manner and on a scale he had wished from the beginning.

He clapped his hands to my shoulders.

"I will show them!" he said, with an intensity of feeling that startled me even in that highly emotional encounter.

He told me he understood our arrangements and approved of them. True, he had already let copies of *The First Circle* out of his hands, but only to trusted friends. He said that he was certain he could retrieve them and would do so. As for my suggestion that he could, if necessary, denounce the publication of *The First Circle*, he said emphatically that he would *never* do this. Looking back, I now interpret his certainty on this point—a year before the publication of this novel and *Cancer Ward*—to have meant that Solzhenitsyn had by then assessed his own forces and those of his antagonists, measured the effect of his surprise flank attack from the West, and been confident that he would prevail. Though a number of Western journalists were to read statements of his, notably those he made in 1968 about *Cancer Ward*, as a condemnation of the publication of *The First Circle*, to my knowledge no such disclaimer was ever made by him. In the case of the book he had called "his life," he did not intend to demonstrate the slightest subservience to Soviet authority. He had no intention of taking the path Pasternak had been induced to follow after *Dr. Zhivago* appeared. In no way would he diminish the effect of its publication around the world. His books were to appear as inevitable events of a higher Russian destiny. From now on, attack and defense were to be identical: a series of calculated, supremely well-timed publications, letters to the authorities, statements, news conferences. Attack. Attack again. And later there would be yet another book—an immensely important one about Russia's buried history. Between our meetings that spring and fall, his overall battle plan had become in his mind a reality; the campaign had begun even before his enemies sensed on what ground the battle would be fought. Or its magnitude.

Before we went back inside I told Solzhenitsyn that I was not leaving Russia for a few days yet. He could reflect on what I had said. We could talk again.

No, he told me, there would be no need to meet again now. We were in agreement. The plan was to be carried out without delay and, he repeated, he would never repudiate it. As we started back into the room he took my arm again and spoke to me with a warmth and exaltation that swept away all my uncertainties: "We are involved together in an unheard of adventure. You may not be able to return to Russia—it could be dangerous for you and for me. But in my heart I feel that we shall meet again some day. It can't be otherwise."

When we went inside I felt enormous relief. Now we could proceed with the publication of *The First Circle* with the certainty that Solzhenitsyn would stand behind us.

7

THE NEXT MORNING, in my hotel room at the Metropole, the first elation of having accomplished the objective of the trip began to fade as Solzhenitsyn's words, "You may not be able to return to Russia," came back to me. They revived my forebodings, and I thought of which friends I could still see in Moscow without too great a risk of compromising them.

One was Ernst Neizvestny.

The studio of the sculptor, on Sergeevsky Lane, was a center of intellectual life in Moscow. Everyone went there, Muscovites and Moscow-wise foreign visitors alike. Neizvestny, whom I had first met in 1960, was in his mid-forties, one of the few Soviet artists who was struggling to keep his professional integrity while remaining involved in the official artistic activities of Moscow. The sculptor's life was a constant battle with the leaders of the

Artists Union, the reactionary organization that controls every aspect of an artist's career in the USSR. A born fighter who had earned numerous military distinctions in World War II, Neizvestny usually managed to hold his own with the Union. In 1962 he had been one of the artists with whom Nikita Khrushchev had raucously argued during the dramatic confrontation in the Manège exhibition hall. Subsequently, Khrushchev had befriended Neizvestny, whose shrewdness and forcefulness had appealed to the Soviet leader.

Neizvestny's work—projects for monumental government commissions (most, once Khrushchev fell from power, never to be realized), small bronzes, and magnificent, elaborate drawings and etchings—is based on his violent experiences as a soldier. At one time he survived in a punishment battalion assigned to neutralize a mine field by running through it. He was intensely aware of the sufferings undergone by Russians in concentration camps, of the world of Gulag, where many of his relatives and friends— Neizvestny is half Jewish—had disappeared in the late forties. Gulag provided some of his more obsessive themes, yet he would not acknowledge publicly the importance of Soviet concentration camp experience in his work, for to have done so would have caused him to lose all hope for state patronage. At that time, Solzhenitsyn's and Sakharov's grand strategy of the intellectual stepping forward as "another government" of Russia was not yet conceivable, even for a man of Neizvestny's strength.

In 1967 this liberal and "modern" artist who did not clash openly with proponents of Socialist Realism was a celebrity in the USSR. Because of his numerous contacts with the West, he was regarded as suspect by the authorities. There was an atmosphere of threat around his studio. Despite this, it was visited almost every day by fellow artists from all parts of Russia and by others from abroad. Gregarious by nature, the sculptor had to be on constant alert against informers sent there by the authorities to keep an eye on him and his guests.

It would be well known that I had called on Neizvestny on all my trips to Moscow. One more visit—perhaps my last—would do no great harm.

To stop by his studio was to enter a world with a mysterious life of its own. Empty lots surrounded the decrepit, turn-of-the-century building, recalling certain torn-down sections of lower Manhattan in the early sixties. To be let in, one knocked loudly in the agreed-upon fashion on the old rusty shutters, which the sculptor kept locked with a chain and a huge padlock as a precaution against *drushinniky*, the hoodlums in government pay who were beginning to harass outspoken members of the liberal intelligentsia. I knocked. Neizvestny came to the door and peered through the shutters. Heavyset, broad-shouldered, full of physical energy, he unchained the shutters and ushered me in with shushing gestures and much pointing up to the ceiling. I entered what once had been a small shop, now jammed with hundreds of statues, the walls covered with drawings of figures in motion, of strange masks and machines. In the tense atmosphere of those days, the studio seemed peaceful, a dark sanctuary of gray clay and bronze.

He showed me a series of drawings of giants who embodied cosmic forces in conflict, the elemental pitted against the mechanized in mythical battle scenes. As I looked at the drawings, I recalled a conversation we had had that spring. I had asked Neizvestny why he never recorded everyday life in his work. There was so much that was visually exciting in Moscow then— the faces of people, the streets where old and new clashed, the ominous May Day parades with their displays of weaponry. I had cited Solzhenitsyn. In *One Day*, the hero's experiences throughout his day in camp are immediate, tangible. Should not this clear rendition of reality be achieved in the visual arts also? Wasn't Solzhenitsyn on the right track?

Neizvestny had answered that he admired Solzhenitsyn as a writer with an enormous capacity for work, as a strong and courageous man, but could it not be that his art was old-fashioned? Russia had no need of more traditionalists. As a sculptor,

Neizvestny aspired to become a significant artist on an international scale.

In the discussion that followed, I, a Westerner, had defended Solzhenitsyn and the idea of realism in art, while Neizvestny, a Soviet, had spoken for philosophical abstraction.

Now, as we talked of the new drawings and of the philosophy of art, I avoided the subject of Solzhenitsyn. But on that afternoon, for Neizvestny none other would hold his attention.

He offered me tea in a mustard glass—the sculptor cared little for the amenities of life—and the conversation turned to the one subject I felt I should avoid and yet which most absorbed me.

Neizvestny had just finished reading *The First Circle*.

How many copies, I wondered, were circulating in the city? Neizvestny and Solzhenitsyn were not personally acquainted, though they had a number of friends in common.

He said it was a large-scale, powerful book, far more dangerous to its author than either *One Day* or *Cancer Ward*.

"Fantastic!" he said. "A tremendous book! One chapter called 'The Troika of Liars' catches the whole essence of Soviet life. The chapters on Stalin are magnificent. *The First Circle* is a major work of art."

"Not provincial?" I asked.

"No!" he said. "It has existential depth." Then, intent on making me understand, he said, "There's a Jewish belief that if a country has seven just men it will be saved. Now Russia has two: Alexander Solzhenitsyn and Andrei Sakharov." He smiled, adding, "Only five to go."

Years later I was to learn that while we spoke that day in the studio on Sergeevsky Lane, a copy of *The First Circle* was hidden in one of Neizvestny's sculptures, sealed inside the large cast-iron head of "The Young Worker" which then dominated the studio.

An hour later, as I was about to leave, Neizvestny showed me some of his recent etchings. They were expressionistic figures representing human emotions, inspired by themes from Dostoyevsky, his favorite novelist.

"Berger must have them," he told me. "I want you to take them to him."

John Berger was a mutual friend, an English art critic and novelist, who was then writing a book on Neizvestny. I hesitated. Nothing must interfere with my mission for Solzhenitsyn. I told Neizvestny about having been searched on the spring trip.

"Nitchevo, never mind," he assured me. "I'll give you a number, someone to call if they give you any trouble. He'll straighten it out."

Then it struck me that it might be a good idea to have something to divert the KGB's attention should they somehow suspect my real reason for being in Russia.

"I'll take them," I told him, "but give me that number. I have a feeling I'll need it."

On a corner of one of the etchings he wrote a name and a phone number. He told me that it was a high official of Novosti, the Soviet news agency.

Neizvestny walked me all the way back to the Metropole. Along the bent streets, the block of leveled rubble, past the Kremlin, to the Bolshoi Plaza, where the hotel stands. It was another beautiful, unseasonably warm day. We passed people returning from the country, animated and suntanned, carrying baskets of mushrooms and apples. As we approached the Metropole, Neizvestny let me know that he did not want to be seen in the hotel with a foreigner. We would say good-bye in the public garden in the plaza, among red geraniums and girls in summer dresses. A sedate version of the miniskirt was the fashion that year, giving Moscow a carefree "Western" look.

Neizvestny was giving me various verbal messages for John Berger. As we talked, we moved toward the monument of Karl Marx that sits in the center of the garden. I knew that Neizvestny passionately hated this statue, erected in the early sixties by some academic hack, a monument to the arrested state of Soviet art.

In midsentence Neizvestny glanced up, glaring at the massive, neckless head of Marx which stared gloomily out from a cube of stone, as if brooding on the sorry fate of being sculpted by the worst sculptor in the world.

"Damnation!" Neizvestny exclaimed quite loudly, brandishing the roll of etchings at the Father of Socialism. "When I think that foreigners judge our country by such abominations! Some night I'll get drunk and smash it into a million pieces!" He waved the etchings menacingly.

I had the feeling that we were being watched. A girl in a short red summer dress was edging nearer, keeping her eyes averted. I thought I recognized her as an employee of the Metropole, which could mean that she was in the pay of the police. Neizvestny read my look. He handed me the etchings and we said hasty farewells.

"A million pieces," he added in a low voice as we parted.

Quickly I crossed the plaza and walked into the Metropole, holding the etchings close to my side.

On my last visit to Chukovsky I came by electric train to a Peredelkino bathed in tender autumn light, lovelier than I had ever seen it, yet somehow unreal, dreamlike in the softly dying Indian summer, known in Russian as "country woman's summer."

I went first to the cemetery on the hill. Chukovsky's wife is buried there. My maternal grandmother, Olga Elsyeevna Kolbassin Chernov, has lain there since 1965. She is buried near a big gray rock, close to the three pines which mark the grave of Pasternak. I put the purple-red asters I had bought at a Moscow street market near her gravestone, mixing them with rust-colored and pale green leaves. Bright hues had always pleased her—"as much as music," she had said. Pasternak's grave I found strewn with chrysanthemums and apples, a fragrant, pagan homage to a poet who had loved life.

On the way to Chukovsky's, I walked by Pasternak's house. It looked deserted, haunted with sadness. The poet's small garden, which he had tilled himself, was no longer cultivated. I looked back up to the cemetery, across the lyrical landscape that Pasternak had delighted in, the broad, freshly plowed field rising to the small blue-cupolated church, the three pines. In the pale sun it looked ethereal, a vision of Russia that one was awakening from, leaving.

> *It has cleared its way*
> *And stares from the hill*
> *Winter*
> *Upon my life through the frightened yellow leaves.*

When I reached Chukovsky's house nearby, he was still resting. The housekeeper showed me into the dining room. I sat there alone looking at the drawings on the deep blue walls; one was a brilliant caricature of Chukovsky—Mayakovsky's work, I believe—dated 1912, showing his fluent hands, the odd twist of his nose in his long, fleshy face. When my host came in, he looked not very different from his portrait as a young man of thirty.

He knew that I was leaving Moscow the next day and that I had come to say good-bye. He was determined that our parting should not be a melancholy one. First he saw to it that I was served a bite to eat—some kasha with freshly pickled mushrooms, a glass of homemade kvass. Then we went for our usual walk. Chukovsky joked incessantly, clowning to keep sadness from coming between us. His antics had the opposite effect on me. I felt a mounting sense of sorrow as we strolled along the familiar lanes in the late afternoon. Why had my life to be split between worlds at odds with each other? Would our work for Solzhenitsyn help to bring these worlds closer or would it only create more fear and estrangement? Why couldn't I talk about Solzhenitsyn's request with this friend of my grandfather's, the one person in Russia who could best understand and advise me in the task that weighed on me? I felt an almost irresistible impulse to confide in him, this wizard who could make a lion and my grandfather talk in "live voices," who could pull the past out of his hat. He knew Solzhenitsyn well. He knew Russia and the West. He adored my parents. He could perhaps throw some light on what was best to do. Magicians like him make it their business to know the future too.

I kept silent. To speak of the secret, even to Solzhenitsyn's friend would have been a violation of trust; a violation also of the rules we had set ourselves for Solzhenitsyn's safety.

And too, I remembered Chukovsky's warning: "Don't get involved; you are a fine journalist, keep yourself free to move between Russia and the West—what you have to contribute in the realm of East-West contacts cannot be duplicated." Perhaps he knew much already and kept silent because he disapproved, or preferred to remain aloof. Or perhaps he knew nothing and would have caught fire from Solzhenitsyn's daring plan, perhaps danced a jig in the lanes of Peredelkino. I would never know.

After a cup of tea at the house, I said good-bye to Chukovsky in his garden. It was dusk. I started down the darkening lane in the direction of the railway station, the three pines and the church cupola faintly silhouetted against the greenish evening sky. Glancing back, I saw Chukovsky's tall figure at the gate. He waved his long arms, blew a kiss, then, as I waved to him, turned back into the garden. I felt a sharp sense of loss. I knew that I would never see him again.

THE DAY of my departure was misty but still extremely warm. As in the spring, I arrived at the airport shortly before my morning flight was due to depart, in order to spend the least time in the company of police and customs officials.

It was odd to be leaving Moscow without having visited so many close friends and relatives. I felt that I had only arrived yet already had to go. Such were the demands of this new life. I was no longer responsible only to myself. Others' safety had to be considered—best to leave at once. I had cabled Henry: TRIP COMPLETELY SUCCESSFUL LEAVING MOSCOW TODAY LOVE.

But I was not yet out of Russia.

Entering the crowded customs area I found that there was a snag. What had been a light mist in town was a blanket of fog at Sheremetyevo. All departures were delayed or canceled—mine, via Vienna, for three hours. The terminal was a madhouse; parties of tourists who were to have left early that morning overflowed the main hall; Swedes and Germans milled around, trading apples and bottles of vodka, a noisy crowd. They seemed to be celebrating the end of their Russian visit, and their exuberance upset the Soviet airport personnel. Everyone was supposed to check in at once and wait—all day if necessary—in the bleak lounge beyond the police and customs areas.

Exactly what I wanted to avoid. Remembering my search the previous spring, I had no intention of offering the officials any more time than necessary to study me and my luggage and perhaps make telephone inquiries. On the spur of the moment I decided to take a cab to a well-known Moscow landmark not far from the airport, the palace of Ostankino.

Since there was no way to check my suitcase without checking in myself, I deposited it by a pillar near the check-in counter. No one would take it—and even if they did I had nothing of value except Neizvestny's etchings, and they were one of several sets. All that mattered to me then was that I escape the oppressive bedlam of the airport, the cruising eyes of the officials. And a rising sense of claustrophobia: Whatever desire I had had to linger on in Moscow was gone.

A five-minute cab ride and I was at Ostankino, the eighteenth-century palace built by the Count Sheremetiev for the beautiful young actress-serf Parasha, who had become his wife and died soon afterward. Built of wood stuccoed to resemble stone, the palace aspires to be a Roman villa; in the hazy sun it looked more like a Jean Cocteau movie set, with outsized busts on short pillars before an enchanting, neoclassic façade. In the gardens, roses were still in bloom. I walked the grounds of Ostankino oblivious of everything but this enchanted retreat until the sun burned the haze away.

I was back at the airport by twelve. The confusion had subsided. My suitcase stood where I had left it, and I took it to the check-in counter and produced my passport.

The young man who took it glanced once; then very suddenly he shouted at me in Russian, "Where were you? You had no right to leave the area. You're breaking the law. You should have checked in this morning." While he shouted he was summoning two other functionaries, who instantly became as agitated as he. Putting my suitcase on a counter they opened it and groped through my loosely packed skirts, blouses, underwear, nightgown, then dumped everything out. Two elderly Frenchmen checking in nearby looked on, startled and sympathetic. My clothing lay in a disorderly pile with Neizvestny's etchings, which I had laid on the bottom of the suitcase, now on top. I decided that the time had come to make a little speech.

"Comrades," I said, as calmly as I could, "why do you make a spectacle of yourselves in front of foreigners? What will they think of the Soviet Union? I have broken no law. I am checking in a whole half-hour before the rescheduled departure for Vienna. These Frenchmen will think that Soviet officials are boorish."

This had the effect of slowing them down. One of them said, "Petka, she's right. The foreigners are ogling us." They shoved my possessions back into the suitcase, which now overflowed. One of the officials cradled it, open, in his arms and carried it out through a side door. I was told to follow. I found myself in a small, windowless room furnished with a table and one metallic chair in a corner. I sat on the chair and tried to remain collected, while, once again, the three officials emptied out my bag on the table and studied its contents, especially Neizvestny's etchings.

Now the first official was questioning me. Why was I so late in checking in? There had been an important comrade waiting here especially to talk to me. Now he was gone, called away on business elsewhere. They were under orders to interrogate me about my activities in Russia. But first: What were these obscene drawings doing in my bag? Did I trade in pornography? Did I know that it was against regulations? The young man was waving the etchings in my face with an expression of profound disgust.

I believe that Niezvestny's etchings saved me from a more searching interrogation. Those expressionistic representations of emotions, only vaguely suggesting human forms, excited the airport officials' prurient imaginations. They forgot their "important comrade's" order to find out about my activities in Russia. They took turns leafing through the prints, exchanging lewd remarks. It was ridiculous. Yet time was running out and I was beginning to feel threatened.

At last I managed to press on the first functionary the name and phone number of the Novosti official Neizvestny had given me. I said that my flight was leaving in twenty minutes and that they would be the ones in trouble if I missed it. The young man went off to telephone, saying over his shoulder, "You won't get me to believe that this is art. This is pornography meant to dishonor our country! You will not get away with it!"

When he had gone I became more and more tense. Would the official be there to answer the phone? What if he was out to lunch? Might I be let on the plane before the three remembered that they had to check on my activities in Moscow?

Unexpected relief came in the person of a middle-aged man who had quietly entered the room. He was red-haired with a ruddy Russian peasant's face, perhaps a senior customs employee, and he acted less like a policeman than the others. He seemed surprised by the commotion, by the scattered lingerie and the etchings. I sat as calmly as I could on the metal chair, trying to look both innocent and offended. I decided to appeal to the newcomer.

"Comrade, my flight for Vienna is about to leave. These people are behaving like savages. Please see to it that I don't miss my plane. They think those etchings are subversive. They are works of art by a distinguished member of the Artists Union."

At that moment the young man who had gone off to telephone returned, visibly deflated. The Novosti official had confirmed that I had been asked officially to take Neizvestny's prints to the West.

That was enough. Brushing the three younger men aside, the red-haired customs official started repacking my suitcase. He motioned me to help him. We packed everything, including the "pornographic" etchings, back into the suitcase and he forced the lid shut. Without a word he took my passport and ticket from the first young man and disappeared, bringing them back in no more than a minute, stamped. The three younger officials had hurried away. Before I knew it the older man was carrying my bag, marching me quickly down long, windowless airport corridors. He opened a door, handing me my suitcase, pointed to a waiting jet, its engines already accelerating shrilly. The air was filled with the smell of kerosene, a promise of imminent departure, of freedom. Blinded by the sun, I ascended the rear steps into the airplane, stopped halfway, and turned to wave a thank-you to the red-haired man; but he was gone. Seconds after I entered the plane, the door clumped shut behind me.

I was the last passenger to board the flight to Vienna.

FOUR

Point of No Return

How frightening it is
                    when the sky stands still
in the fiery runways
of fantastic cities!
                    —*Andrei Voznesensky,*
                    "New York Airport at Night"

WHEN MY Swissair flight touched down at Kennedy airport on a late October night I was irrevocably committed to seeing through the publication of *The First Circle*. All summer our plans and preparations had seemed tentative, subject to possible change or cancellation. Now, with the author's full approval and a target date—Christmas 1968—I felt an extreme sense of urgency. I realized that the period before publication would be the most dangerous to Solzhenitsyn and that nothing must delay the appearance of the novel.

In Europe I had seen the man who in the spring had handed me the film canisters and warned me about the dangers of what we were undertaking. Excitedly—with some defensiveness—I had told him about my conversation on the balcony and about our determination to proceed. I had expected him to repeat his warnings. Instead he seemed to catch fire from my enthusiasm and, through me, Solzhenitsyn's.

"Of course," he had said, "it must be done. I shall help you in any way I can. *The First Circle* is a masterpiece and should be treated as such."

On the drive home from the airport, I told Henry about my conversation on the balcony and Solzhenitsyn's agreement to our plans, about his enthusiasm. Only once during that drive, when Henry said in passing that the novel could not be published at Christmas, since December was the worst month which to publish a book, did I sense again the gap between Russian and Western perceptions, sense the difficulties that lay ahead. I was not yet on American time.

Soon after my return we started living a triple life, one which we were to lead for many years. On a reduced scale we pursued our usual activities, seeing friends occasionally at night, visiting Michael at boarding school. At that time the main preoccupation of many of our acquaintances was opposition to the war in Vietnam. Though we shared this position and even joined an organization of clergy and laymen against the war in Vietnam, we must have appeared self-absorbed to our activist friends.

The second part of our lives that winter was preparing the novel for publication. We met often with Tom and Harrison, discussing the latest information from the USSR that reached us through open and private channels. We tried to assess how events might affect Solzhenitsyn. With Tony, we were busy working out the terms of a contract with Harper & Row that would both affirm our relationship with Solzhenitsyn, the basis for Harper &

Row's world copyright, and safeguard the secrecy of that relationship. Not an easy task from a legal point of view. I remember that the conversations on this subject, in Connecticut and in Tony's office, again tested my faith in the "big book" approach. While approving of it wholeheartedly, Tony made its risks clear to us. I imagined myself on the witness stand, lips sealed, going to jail.

We often saw Cass and Alan Schwartz, an attorney for Harper & Row. Our intention was to plan all aspects of the publication in advance, while delaying the signing of the contract as long as possible. We wanted to give Solzhenitsyn every opportunity to alter or cancel his instructions. All of us continued to be concerned about the possibility of another manuscript of *The First Circle* surfacing in the West and of the rival claims that would doubtlessly then ensue. In such a case, to defend our claim we might have to make disclosures that could hurt Solzhenitsyn. I had gathered from what Neizvestny had told me about the growing number of underground manuscripts of the novel in circulation that the possibility was very real. In our meetings, Cass and Alan would inquire what we were prepared to do in this event. They asked questions in a polite but tense tone which I found unsettling. The answer was that, ultimately, we would be powerless to do anything: We could in no event endanger Solzhenitsyn's life. Remembering his own assurances and his optimism, I tried to reassure Cass and Alan—and ourselves—as best I could. We must press on with the translation, follow the author's instructions to the letter.

It was at this time that Henry and I came more and more to appreciate Tom Whitney's human and professional qualities and to recognize the full extent of his value as a member of the secret circle. Tom gave all his time and his passion to *The First Circle* during these months, sacrificing everything else in his life. In the Victorian barn converted into a Russian library where he has his study, he would spend ten or twelve hours at his desk translating; and he was always available to us as an adviser as well as a thoughtful friend.

Tom was always conscious of the risks involved in keeping a manuscript of *The First Circle* in his barn. He had an electronic alarm installed. At night he would lock the manuscript and his work in a safe. To his menagerie of horses, cats, and otters, were added several very fierce trained police dogs.

As the days progressed, the third level of our altered lives became especially absorbing. This was our work as editors on the translation of *The First Circle*. We were discovering the richness and breadth of the novel, the special world it created, the variety of its characters, its awesome architecture (which Heinrich Böll was to compare with that of a cathedral), above all, the strength that burst from its pages. Like Tom, we were drawn into that world, deeply affected by it. We felt we knew as intimates Gleb Nerzhin, Solzhenitsyn's alter ego; Lev Rubin, one of the strongest creations in modern Russian literature, the *zek* who despite all he has experienced and witnessed remains loyal to his ideals of communism, bound like Job to his faith; Sologdin, the Nietzschean *zek*, with his Old Russian longings, a camp veteran who draws inspiration from the rigors of his life and his austere code of survival; Spiridon, the janitor who embodies the ancestral Russian peasant virtues; Volodin, the diplomat, a decent man who plummets from the crest of his career into Gulag; Stalin himself, whose shrewd madness Solzhenitsyn portrays with astonishing insight. These and all the other characters of the story lived with us in our house in the woods. We came to know every room in the Mavrino *sharashka*, the scientific institution employing political prisoners as research workers on specially assigned projects. Our house itself became a *sharashka*.

For a while I had Solzhenitsyn-induced dreams. I remember one, very frightening, which I had on a cold, windless, moonlit night that winter. I dreamed that Solzhenitsyn was hiding somewhere inside our darkened house. Red Army soldiers in Russian civil war uniforms and pointed, cloth-covered helmets were surrounding the house, silently closing in on it, their steel bayonets glittering in the moonlight, their long black shadows moving relentlessly toward my window. Now they were breaking into the house; I could hear the heavy sound of their boots, the clanking of their weapons.

I woke up in terror. Everything was silent in the house. I looked out the window. For an endless moment I thought I saw the men in pointed helmets among the moonlit tree trunks outside. The shadows cast by the trees onto the terrace were brilliant black and seemed to be creeping toward me. The terror would not subside. I took the dream as a portent and wondered whether something dreadful was happening to Solzhenitsyn at that moment. Was he in trouble as a result of some miscalculation we had made, or because our activities had been discovered? I could not go back to sleep that night.

More than ever we were worried about possible Soviet surveillance. In the fictional world of *The First Circle*, where many of the characters are engaged in perfecting Stalin's system of electronic spying, no one escapes the dragnet of the secret police. Innokenty Volodin is apprehended after a conversation of only a few seconds over a public telephone. Our activity was undoubtedly of far more interest to Soviet authorities than Volodin's telephone call would have been; and since my spring meeting with Solzhenitsyn, I felt certain that I had left a trail of clues that, if detected and pieced together, could be used to build a case against him.

We did not fully measure at the time how skillfully Solzhenitsyn himself was manipulating the entire Soviet power establishment to work against itself, confusing it with audacious counterattacks, miring it in debate and indecision, fighting a successful holding operation until the day the world publication of his novels—and, unknown to us then, of *The Gulag Archipelago*—would bring him the power a great writer commands, that of being "another government."

Because we were aware what an important book *The First Circle* was, we were anxious to let Cass Canfield have a firsthand sampling of it. For the sake of secrecy we could not engage a typist and we were unwilling to slow our forward motion on the editing to retype the earlier chapters. Henry hit on the idea of recording the first chapter on tape and inviting Cass to the country to listen to it. Cass accepted. I believe that at this juncture, after hearing our reports and Harrison's, he would have traveled halfway around the world for such a reading.

It was early afternoon, a foggy late fall day. Cass sat in Henry's chair, his face in half-silhouette against the already winter-stripped birches outside the windows. Henry pushed the tape recorder's Play button. As he did this I suddenly remembered being inside that sound truck at Chukovsky's, listening to my grandfather's voice, "Andreyev's live voice." Like his, this voice seemed live, yet it also came from another world. From the first it was not Henry's, it was Solzhenitsyn's, instantly recognizable.

"The fretwork hands stood at five to five. In the dying light of the December day the bronze face of the clock on the shelf looked black."

I glanced at Cass. He had stopped breathing.

The first chapter of *The First Circle* describes a single event. Innokenty Volodin, a young member of the diplomatic service, decides to make a phone call to warn an acquaintance, a professor of medicine, that the professor must not deliver a certain package to foreigners. But a trap has been set for the young diplomat. He is aware of the risk in what he is doing but decides he must do the right thing. He goes to a pay phone, places the call, tries to get the warning across. Before he hangs up, the connection is broken.

The scene is developed stroke by stroke, simply, starkly. Listening, I thought of the urgent phone calls that had summoned me to my first meetings with Solzhenitsyn. Cass was transfixed. Through the translation, Solzhenitsyn's voice was reaching him too.

"He was still hesitating—wondering where he could phone without having someone outside the booth rap the glass with a coin. . . . But all this didn't matter any more. . . . If one is forever cautious, can one remain a human being?"

When the tape ended, Henry shut off the machine. For a moment none of us said a word. I had the impression that Cass wanted to get to a phone himself, to take action, to set wheels in motion—until he remembered that we were bound by Solzhenitsyn's schedule, that the translation was a long way from finished, and that publication was more than a year away. He glanced at the stacks of manuscript on Henry's desk.

"There's no doubt," he said then. "It's even more than I'd imagined. The man is a master."

Cass's reaction made us feel more strongly than ever that time was running against us. Others would also recognize the novel's importance and, with who knew how many other manuscripts in circulation, the chances of a rushed and botched unauthorized translation seemed very likely. Yet, along with Tom, we kept working on the five hundred pages of Russian text as if we had no end of time. The translation had to be the very best possible— we could not cut corners. Instead, we extended our workdays—up to eighteen hours.

Then, late in November, a disquieting report emerged. A message from Europe informed us that a person claiming to have Solzhenitsyn's authorization was dealing directly with an Italian publisher for the publication of *The First Circle*. What did it mean? Had Solzhenitsyn not understood the terms of the arrangement he had so enthusiastically approved? Was the person a plant of the KGB trying to smoke out the truth about any publication plans involving Solzhenitsyn's manuscripts? Was the Italian publisher floating the story to stake a claim while another translation was in progress? Or was the story merely someone's invention? Another possibility was painful to consider: Could Solzhenitsyn be deliberately circumventing our arrangements? Remembering the spirit of my last meeting with him, and what Solzhenitsyn had said then, I ruled this out.

The theory of a misunderstanding on Solzhenitsyn's part seemed persuasive enough for us to check out. This meant that once again, so soon after my Moscow meeting, we would have to communicate with him. To proceed toward a contract with Harper & Row in the face of this new uncertainty was too dangerous. We weighed possible means of transmitting inquiries and receiving his response. This time we had to confirm beyond any doubt that he understood, *in Western terms*, all the legal and commercial implications of world publication. Yet he and I had agreed that any further direct contact between us was far too hazardous. We had to take into account the worsening of his position vis-à-vis the Soviet authorities.

Indeed, all that fall, his struggle with the Writers Union had been intensifying. Konstantin Fedin and other members of the literary establishment were demanding that Solzhenitsyn protest the alleged anti-Soviet exploitation in the West of his letter calling for an end to censorship in the USSR. Solzhenitsyn was counterdemanding that the Writers Union secure the return of his "arrested" manuscripts and archives, that they defend him against slander concerning his war record. His publisher, Tvardovsky, despite his immense dedication, was not in a position to support him effectively.

How were we to reach him now, a third time, with a complicated message to which we needed a response, when every day he was being cast more inextricably in the role of "enemy of the people" —and, we were certain, watched constantly? Had we known that he was then finishing *The Gulag Archipelago*, the book that would be most dangerous to him, we would have been even more uneasy.

In the last days of November we learned that a trusted friend would soon be traveling to Moscow. We were certain that this person would be capable of carrying out the delicate mission without compromising Solzhenitsyn. After securing our friend's agreement to assist us in this matter, we began preparing for Solzhenitsyn a new schematic presentation of the world publication plan.

In mid-December, Henry flew to Europe to brief our friend thoroughly on the verbal message that he would bring to Solzhenitsyn.

I settled down to wait for the answer.

9

WITH HENRY IN EUROPE and movement on the Solzhenitsyn project temporarily slowed, I felt as if I were suspended in a surrealistic twilight. Seeking something more solid, I went to New York to stay with close Russian friends.

There, on a rainy day, my friend Jean Vandenheuvel phoned to say that Robert Kennedy wanted to see me to continue the talk we had begun when I had acted as interpreter during his meeting with Yevtushenko.

One heard it said then that a change was taking place in the slain president's brother. The tough politician was showing a serious, searching side. In fact, on that first encounter in 1966 I had seen a glimmer of the "new" Robert Kennedy. He had struck me as being eager to understand points of view and ideas that, one gathered, had not interested him before. One felt that he had perceived a lesson in his brother's life and death. He seemed to be recreating himself from within, in tune with the moral reappraisal the country was embarked upon, as a statesman for the times. I had been impressed by him.

So, when Jean called, I was pleased. And I also saw the meeting as an opportunity to talk to him about Solzhenitsyn. If I could explain his struggle against Soviet authority, give some idea of his importance, then Solzhenitsyn would, I believed, have a powerful voice in the United States to speak for him should he be arrested.

Jean and I were to meet the senator after dinner at the "21" Club. The rain had stopped; it was a mild evening. It felt good to be with a friend, walking in the dusky, shimmering city.

The senator greeted us warmly as we entered the restaurant, which was not yet crowded. We ordered drinks and hamburgers and began to chat about inconsequential things. Gradually, the tables near us filled. It became noisy and people, recognizing Kennedy, began to come up to him. Jean had to leave and, after a while, Kennedy invited me to continue our talk over a nightcap at his apartment.

The night was so warm that we walked. As we neared the East River and the United Nations Plaza, where the Kennedys had an apartment, my thoughts were on Solzhenitsyn. I remembered the Plaza of the Three Railway Stations, where, just after my first meeting with him, I had started to run in the dark. Again, I had the feeling that I no longer belonged to myself as an individual, that now only our mission mattered, that in the peaceful New York night the soaring buildings by the river were only a backdrop for its successful accomplishment. In spirit I was back in Moscow.

We entered the high-ceilinged darkened entrance hall. In the apartment Kennedy turned on the lights in the large living room with its overstuffed couches and chairs covered with flowered chintz, picking up the colors of splashy neo-Impressionist paintings on the walls. We sat in the senator's small, comfortable study. All around me I could make out books and framed photographs of political occasions, meetings, ceremonies of power. There was a portrait of John Kennedy, his smile open and self-confident.

Robert Kennedy made us drinks and sat down facing me. First we spoke of Yevtushenko, who the year before had so intrigued Kennedy—and also annoyed him with tactless questions about his brother's assassination. We talked about the political situation and the spread of *samizdat* in Russia. I told him something about the liberal movement there and about my last trip to the USSR. I said that I had seen two worlds: the world of Moscow and Leningrad, which foreign visitors see, and the vast countryside off the tourist routes, devastated by a half century of exploitation and neglect, where the majority of Russian people suffer from demoralization and decay. Russia as presented by Intourist. Russia as it is.

I told him that one writer in the Soviet Union now wrote powerfully and truthfully about Russia as it is. Alexander Solzhenitsyn.

Had he perhaps heard of the author of *One Day in the Life of Ivan Denisovich*?

From the senator's blank look I realized that he had not.

To this day I remember the growing physical tension which I felt as I tried to project my feelings about the *zek* from Ryazan. I feared that Robert Kennedy shared the liberal American wish to look at the political system in the USSR in positive terms, the "we have our weaknesses too" fallacy.

Still I persisted. I had no idea when I would see Kennedy again and at any moment Solzhenitsyn might need his intervention. My host listened with an amused smile, not at all unfriendly, but he was obviously more impressed by my ardor than by what I was saying.

When I rose to leave, Kennedy said, "Before we meet next, I'll make sure to read that man—what's his name—"

"Solzhenitsyn. Alexander Solzhenitsyn."

"—because I hope this is one of many talks about Russia." He went to a corner of the library and took a book from a cardboard box. "In the meantime," he continued, showing me the book with a photograph of himself on the jacket, "you'll have to read —me."

I read the title: *To Seek a Newer World*. He took the book under a light, inscribed it, and gave it to me, closed.

"With best wishes to you and those Russian writers you talk about so eloquently," he said.

As we left the apartment with its broad glittering view of the East River, the tensions I had felt earlier in our conversation were gone. At the street entrance we said good-bye warmly and the senator helped me into a taxi, waving as it pulled away. In the dim light of the cab, I read the inscription. Imitating Yevtushenko, he had written:

To Olga
who introduced me to "When I go down and see the way some people live and look around dismayed, shame scorches my cheek like the back of a flatiron" and to many others including Sh . . . . sh . . . . sh . . . . .
from her friend Bob Kennedy

I was pleased that though he found Solzhenitsyn's name impossible to pronounce, the senator from New York would surely remember it when next he heard it.

I was never to see Robert Kennedy again. Within a year Alexander Solzhenitsyn's fame would circle the earth, while the young senator, with his acceptance of the challenge to lead his divided country toward a newer world, would be dead.

10

A FEW WEEKS AFTER Henry returned from Europe, we received the report from our emissary. He had met with Solzhenitsyn in Moscow for two and a half hours. The rumor of a separately arranged Italian edition authorized by Solzhenitsyn was false. He had authorized no such edition. The emissary had become convinced that Solzhenitsyn did in fact understand and approve the legal and commercial aspects of world copyright. Throughout the meeting, his enthusiasm had been at a high pitch.

Olga, he had said, could sign the contract with Harper & Row at any time—under no circumstances would he recall the order to publish. Less now than ever did he mean to let the authorities deal with him as they had dealt with Pasternak: He would not be stopped.

According to our emissary, publication should be moved

earlier than the previously agreed upon date of January 1969 (following our advice that it should not come out in December). As early as June if necessary. As for our fears of rival publication, in the three months since my last visit, *samizdat* typists in the USSR had been working around the clock. *The First Circle* was now the talk of Moscow and copies were being smuggled to the West. However, it was not concern over the possibility of competing editions which had led Solzhenitsyn to advance the date of publication but rather the conviction that the time was ripening for the massive attack against the Soviet literary authorities that he was plotting.

"If there is a pirate edition, just proceed as planned," he told our messenger. "Your text is the full and correct one. If need be, I'll recognize yours openly and will sign a letter to that effect."

And then had come staggering news.

One of our messages was to request, if possible, a secret written confirmation of our agreement to be brought by a third person of proved reliability. Solzhenitsyn said that he had no objection in principle but for the present ruled out transmitting a document with his signature as being too dangerous. Later he might find a way. In the meantime, he said that he understood our need to improve our position in the event of a challenge and offered something else: He would be sending us another manuscript, far greater in scope and political importance than *The First Circle*, a nonfiction work twice (it turned out to be closer to three times) the length of the novel. It was a vast essay about the Soviet prison camp system. We would have the manuscript by June. Solzhenitsyn told our emissary we could inform Harper & Row that we would be controlling the rights to this work in exactly the manner we controlled those to *The First Circle* and that in due course Harper & Row would be its publisher. In this way, he said, we could strengthen our relationship with Harper & Row and avoid the need of a document with a compromising signature.

The messenger's report offered clear indications of the magnitude and the literary and historical value of the "labor camp book." It was not to reach us for months, yet from the start, from the way the message was phrased, we sensed that this manuscript might produce the greatest explosion in the forthcoming salvo Solzhenitsyn intended. Still, in the absence of any actual challenge and with all our efforts needed now for the publication of *The First Circle* in a few months, we decided to delay telling Cass much about this work until we had the manuscript in hand and could read and assess it. We told Cass only that we had clear evidence that Alexander Solzhenitsyn wanted me to continue to act as his representative for a new book which would soon be in our possession. At the time, we did not know that its title was *The Gulag Archipelago*.

In MID-FEBRUARY 1968, Tony brought the contracts for *The First Circle* to Connecticut. By then I had set aside the last of my doubts. The report our messenger brought back had been categorical: Solzhenitsyn expected us to act now, to keep to the new schedule, which now called for early fall publication in the United States and, simultaneously, in other Western countries.

The document Tony brought had been carefully drafted by him and Alan Schwartz to provide all parties to it—especially the absent author—with as much protection against eventual challenges as possible. It provided for an advance payment of $62,500 to the author's account if no written authorization naming me as his trustee was received from him before publication; if such a document was received, the advance would be doubled. My signature was to appear only on a separate rider, in order to keep my identity secret from all but Cass and a very few of his trusted associates.

By this time, we had formulated the financial provisions under which we would carry out our work. The problem had been to translate Solzhenitsyn's open-handed yet vague injunctions on the subject of money into terms which would be fair and would also permit us to do the full-time job required. Since Henry was performing the work of a literary agent, he would receive a commission on earnings of *The First Circle*. In addition, we would receive a fee for editorial work on the translation. Out-of-pocket expenses would be reimbursed. I would receive no remuneration as Solzhenitsyn's trustee.

At the earliest opportunity, through trusted messengers, we presented these arrangements to Solzhenitsyn for his approval or rejection. His response, then and later, was always the same: "Let there be no thought of money. Use the earnings freely to advance the project."

The actual signing of the contract is still vivid in my memory. It took place in Henry's study, where we had played for Cass the taped reading of Innokenty Volodin's fateful telephone call. As I reached for the pen, the phone in the living room rang. Henry went to answer it. A minute later he was back. It was for me.

I put the pen down. "Did they say who it was?"

"Comrade Kozlov of the Soviet Mission to the U.N."

The three of us looked at each other. With a sinking heart and thoughts of electronic surveillance reaching from Moscow to Connecticut, I went to the phone.

In Russian, a male voice greeted me with that mixture of arrogance and joviality so typical of junior Soviet officials. The man told me his name and patronymic. Did I not remember him? How could it be? We had met at a reception in honor of the poet Voznesensky.

"I wish, please, to ask a few questions."

"About what?"

"About what we talked about. You do not remember? I told you I was conducting an investigation."

My thoughts raced. What investigation? Dimly I recalled meeting someone called Kozlov a year or more ago. What had we talked about? Could he have mentioned Solzhenitsyn? Could I have said something damaging? The voice on the phone took on an impatient tone.

"Andreyev!" he said. "I told you I was conducting a literary investigation of Andreyev. How could you forget?"

Hearing this, I did not feel in the least relieved. It struck me as being unlikely that the caller's real purpose was to ask questions about my grandfather.

Abruptly I advised the man to look up the excellent analysis of Andreyev's work and career in Dmitri Mirsky's history of Russian literature, a book unavailable, to be sure, in the USSR.

"It is published by Knopf, you can get it anywhere in this country," I said and hung up.

Looking back, I realize that Comrade Kozlov was in fact interested in me as a likely source of information about my grandfather. Things are sometimes what they seem—though with official Soviets, not too often.

I returned to Henry's study. My hand was shaking as I signed the contract for *The First Circle*.

FIVE

Reckless and Irresponsible

11

SPRINGTIME BROUGHT a gradual easing of our tensions. Solzhenitsyn, fighting a complicated war with the Writers Union, was nonetheless surviving in Russia. We were all working hard on the translation of *The First Circle* so as to have it finished in time for September publication. That spring, I spent a lot of time sitting in the sun, checking over the last chapters; even today, certain passages of the book, among the darkest, are joined in my mind with the splendor of that spring in Connecticut. But this relatively tranquil period was deceptive. Shortly, the storms would break.

The battle Solzhenitsyn was fighting was essentially a holding action intended to engage his antagonists in the Writers Union until *The First Circle* and *Cancer Ward* were published in the West—and until *The Gulag Archipelago* could be delivered to us.

The smokescreen was *Cancer Ward*. In response to the repeated demands that he denounce the capitalists' use of his name as a leader of Russian dissenters, Solzhenitsyn condemned the Writers Union for, among other things, its refusal to back the publication of *Cancer Ward* in Russia. The decision of an emigré, anti-Soviet publisher in Germany to issue the book in Russian prompted its author to issue an open letter, dated April 18, 1968, to the Writers Union and to *Novi Mir* and *Literaturnaya Gazeta*:

> This episode compels us to reflect on the terrible and dark avenues by which the manuscripts of Soviet writers can reach the West. It constitutes an extreme reminder to us that literature must not be brought to a state in which literary works become a profitable commodity for any scoundrel who happens to have a travel visa. The works of our authors must be printed in their own country and must not become the plunder of foreign publishing houses.

At one level of meaning—that which would be seized upon by Soviet officials—the "scoundrel" had to be Victor Louis, who was said to have peddled the manuscript of *Cancer Ward* in the West on behalf of the KGB. At that level, the whole letter amounted to an honest blast of outraged Soviet sensibility. Read in its full context, however, the missive is worthy of Gogol. The Inspector General making fools of the entire town. Its hidden satire reveals the relish with which Solzhenitsyn played his cat-and-mouse game with the Soviet establishment at this period, leaving no doubt as to who was cat and who was mouse, who powerful and who weak, who right and who wrong.

That spring we read those words with trepidation. Despite Solzhenitsyn's reassurances, we feared that they might be followed by a specific denunciation of the publication of *The First Circle* once it was publicly announced in June. Solzhenitsyn was never to issue such a denunciation. All his protests were directed elsewhere against the publication of *Cancer Ward*. He kept his promise to me.

Toward the end of spring, as the news of a major novel by Solzhenitsyn was about to be formally announced by the publisher, outcries began to be heard. Harper & Row, it was said, having somehow come into possession of a manuscript, was acting irresponsibly, without regard to the author's safety, in publishing it. We had anticipated such criticism and discussed at great length how Harper & Row was to respond to it. The problem was by no means simple. In balance then were both the safety and interests of Solzhenitsyn, which depended on keeping his authorization of publication secret, and the reputation of a multimillion-dollar publicly owned corporation charged with reckless actions. Both Cass and Alan Schwartz met the challenge skillfully and with sensitivity to the author's position—but it was not easy. On the face of it, there was reason to question Harper & Row's judgment in publishing a novel at a time when the author was vociferously attacking the unprincipled plunderers of his work in the West. Many people of goodwill did question the publisher's motives. There may also have been more complex forces at work.

One hot May afternoon in New York, Henry and I were attending the opening of a show of Neizvestny's works that I had arranged at the sculptor's request. It was taking place at the Sculptors Guild in an old Madison Avenue brownstone that had been converted into a gallery. I was standing in the stuffy upper gallery near one of Neizvestny's disemboweled nudes when a dark-haired good-looking woman I knew slightly came up to me and at once began talking excitedly about Solzhenitsyn. She was Patricia Blake, an authority on Russian literature who with the translator Max Hayward had produced a Mayakovsky anthology. She was then—and is to this day—associated with *Time* magazine as its Russian expert. Excitedly, she urged me to use my influence to stop publication of *The First Circle* by Harper & Row. She denounced greedy publishers who knew nothing of Russian affairs, assuring me that the publication would certainly lead to Solzhenitsyn's death.

"Don't they understand—his life is at stake? We all must take a stand!" she kept repeating.

I remained as noncommittal as possible, all the while wondering if she could possibly know anything of my connection with Solzhenitsyn or whether she was speaking to me simply as another writer on Soviet literary matters. Why did she single me out in this way? There were many people in New York City who were much closer to Cass Canfield than I.

Soon after our encounter in the gallery we learned from Cass that William Collins, the head of the English firm he had licensed to publish *The First Circle* in the United Kingdom, was dissatisfied with the Whitney translation. At first we assumed that the problem was the common one of differences between American and British usage, especially in the renderings of dialogue and labor camp slang, and we agreed that Collins should have a free hand in altering what struck British ears as Americanisms. However it soon appeared that the problem, in Collins's view, lay much deeper than that. Acting on the advice of his own expert, the English publisher was insisting that they would not use the Whitney translation at all and, despite the fact that Solzhenitsyn's target date for publication was only a few months away, they would embark on a new translation of their own.

We protested to Cass and Alan. We were responsible for the quality of the translation, for getting it ready in time to meet the schedule arranged with the author. We knew that if the English translation was in fact to be an original one, there was no way a version of high quality could be produced in time to keep a publication date in September, when all editions were to be published simultaneously.

Cass did what he could to represent us in this matter, but his hands were tied, since he could disclose neither the reasons for our objections nor our identities, only that there *were* objections. Collins remained firm. Cass himself knew and could recommend the Russian expert who was advising Collins and offering his services as translator. He was the principal translator of *Dr. Zhivago*, Max Hayward. He was to work with Michael Glenny and produce a new translation under separate copyright.

To avoid destructive complications we finally accepted the

Collins arrangement as a fait accompli, insisting only that the U.S. edition not be delayed on account of the revised translation under way in England.

In June, Harper & Row formally announced that publication of *The First Circle* would occur in September. That same month, we received word that the manuscript of the "labor camp book" was in the West. We flew to Paris to assume responsibility for Solzhenitsyn's new work, described by the person who brought it out of Russia simply as "Big Fish."

12

IN THE SUMMER OF 1968, the Parisians Henry and I met, like war veterans recounting battles, were telling over and over again the events of their May "revolution," as if, were they to stop talking, the memory of this vernal spree would be lost in the summer haze. The trees along Boulevard St.-Michel had been chopped down by rioting students. The seated statue of Montaigne, once so elegant and thoughtful looking, was now drenched with red paint. The Paris municipal authorities, recognizing the gravity of the situation, had ordered the Rue des Ecoles asphalted, thus ending the centuries-old tradition of students heaving cobblestones at the constabulary. Citizens beginning to leave on their yearly vacations drove off through a city that looked like a reveler the morning after, unkempt and forlorn, astonished at what had happened the night before.

We took charge of *The Gulag Archipelago* and started back for the United States.

On the flight we discussed how to proceed. Our major problem would be security, which we would have to tighten even further, for, with greater international attention focusing on Solzhenitsyn, secrecy would be more difficult to maintain. Even photostating the filmed manuscript would present greater dangers this time. So, too, would securing the English translation. Would Tom agree to undertake this enormous task?

And in the back of both our minds: What would this new and greater responsibility, requiring not one but several years of work, mean to our own lives?

When we arrived in Connecticut, Harrison came to our aid in providing a secure way of photostating the manuscript. He made arrangements for Henry to take the films to a plant in New Jersey, a subsidiary of the *New York Times*, where the work could be done under Henry's supervision. I remember that he went off to New Jersey on a very hot summer day, returning late in the evening with enormously bulky boxes—three copies of *The Gulag Archipelago*, which turned out to be 1,500 pages long.

In the next weeks Tom and I read separate copies of the book. How to describe the impact it had on us! It covered the reigns of both Lenin and Stalin, following every kind of Soviet citizen from arrest through interrogations, sentencing, and into the world of prisons and camps, usually to death there, sometimes to exile or escape, occasionally to release, as in the author's case. No matter how well acquainted one may be with recent Russian history, the enormity of Stalin's penal universe, as recreated by Solzhenitsyn, is breathtaking. No less breathtaking is the literary mastery with which it is written. I spent a good part of the summer reading *Gulag* slowly, absorbing the gigantic epic of the terror that had possessed the country which had been my parents' homeland, and which I felt was in part mine.

I had to take it little by little. The cumulative effect of Solzhenitsyn's recitation is cathartic, but once or twice, reading it, I came as close to a mental breakdown as I have ever been. Even with Solzhenitsyn's literary art, the sheer mass of human suffering and waste is too much for the mind to accept.

Our instructions were that Solzhenitsyn wanted *The Gulag Archipelago* published on his signal, his expectation being that publication would occur within two years. This meant there was no time to lose in proceeding with the English translation and preparing in secret the complex machinery for world publication, including a Russian edition. As had been the case with *The First Circle*, after my initial meeting with its author specific instructions were few. We had a manuscript and a general indication to act for Solzhenitsyn as we had done with the novel, except that, for the present, we were not to proceed beyond an informal understanding with Harper & Row. Questions remained: Was the work—seven sections divided into three parts—to be published as one volume or several? If the latter, were the volumes to be published simultaneously or one by one? How were foreign translations to be arranged for safely? And always: Were there other manuscripts in circulation?

Clearly, further communication with Solzhenitsyn was necessary—but now communication would be riskier than ever. As before, we were in a position to send and receive certain prearranged signals, but to exchange new information and instructions we would have to await suitable opportunities.

When we told Cass and Alan about *The Gulag Archipelago* that summer, they realized at once that the new work would be a publishing project of gigantic scale. They were eager to know when we would be able to contract it. As in the case of *The First Circle*, Harrison corroborated my assessment of the work, calling it the greatest Russian book of our time. I suspect that the news of a forthcoming literary behemoth from Solzhenitsyn sent shock waves through the upper echelons of Harper & Row. The prospect of publishing it added to the authority with which *The First Circle* was handled by Cass that September. This effect, I believe, was precisely what the author intended when he expressly authorized us to tell Harper & Row about the "labor camp book" long before he was ready to put it under contract. Solzhenitsyn's instincts, particularly his sense of timing in such matters, are extraordinary, and never more so than at this period. Despite secrecy, on the eve of publication of *The First Circle*, hints that another major Solzhenitsyn book was to come from Harper & Row may also have crossed the Atlantic, reaching the ears of his English and European publishers.

The best news for us that summer was that Tom Whitney had agreed to proceed at once with the enormous task of translating *The Gulag Archipelago*.

So—for better and for worse—Solzhenitsyn's masterwork entered our lives.

13

BY FALL OF 1968 the need to communicate with Solzhenitsyn had, once again, become pressing.

At this time, highly publicized legal struggles of the kind we had feared would break out over *The First Circle* were in fact disrupting the publication of *Cancer Ward* in the West. There was evidence that this was an intentional spoiling engineered in part by the KGB. Solzhenitsyn had protested the role of Victor Louis in hawking the manuscript in Europe. In the United States, Dial Press and Farrar, Straus & Giroux were bringing out competing editions of the novel. In Paris, the Russian-language YMCA Press, secretly favored by Solzhenitsyn, was unable to persuade other publishers that it had a valid claim to *Cancer Ward*'s world rights. In November, litigation was raging between Dial Press in the United States and Bodley Head in England. It was reported that secret documents were produced before the court to support the Bodley Head claim to *Cancer Ward*.

We realized that this sort of publicity was one thing in the case of the politically benign *Cancer Ward* and quite another in the case of the secretly authorized time bomb in our hands, *The Gulag Archipelago*. We knew that Soviet authorities could not ignore its publication and we wanted its author to have full control of its timing. We needed to let him know that, owing to the length of the manuscript, securing a suitable translation would take time, perhaps a few months longer than he anticipated. But the delay, we believed, would give him as much as another year of freedom in which to write, perhaps another year of life.

Another consideration made immediate contact with Solzhenitsyn imperative. We had been informed that he had written a new version of *The First Circle*, with ten additional chapters and a slightly different plot line, and that he was considering publishing some of those chapters in the West—independently of Harper & Row.

We knew Solzhenitsyn was jubilant about the great success of his novels throughout the world and we had heard, too, that he was grateful for our role in contributing to the success of one of them. ("Words fail me," he was said to have repeated again and again, when referring to our role.) Yet Solzhenitsyn was now giving indications that he cared little about Western legal relationships.

It was at this time, when the author's acknowledgment of our services to his mission was most extravagantly and, we believed, sincerely expressed, that Henry first raised the possibility that a second Solzhenitsyn, different from the man I had spoken with on the balcony on that balmy autumn night, was making his presence felt. Henry glimpsed the supremely adroit *zek* emerging as a man of power, for whom not only legal but also human bonds were Lilliputian contrivances when it came to fulfilling what he viewed as his destiny.

Nevertheless, we could only work in the belief that the man I had met the previous year was still, despite sudden fame, the man we were dealing with. It was in this spirit that we prepared for the next exchange of information with him.

We decided that this time Henry should go to Russia.

As we had done for the previous trips, we carefully rehearsed our complicated message, reducing it to its simplest terms, which could be memorized precisely. To express the concept of the invisible chain on which copyright, contracts, and licenses were based, Henry worked out the following diagrams:

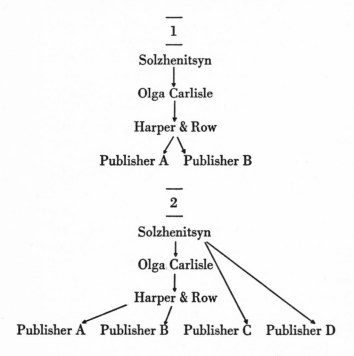

The first showed the relationships established for the publication of *The First Circle*. The second showed the kind of situation we feared would arise if Solzhenitsyn did not understand or did not honor the exclusive trust under which world rights were already contracted to Harper & Row.

Henry flew to Moscow the first week of November 1968, ar-

riving late at night, his Swissair Caravelle homing in on the red
star atop Sheremetyevo. His visit was planned to coincide with
the annual celebration of the Revolution, when a great deal of
wild drinking takes place and the vigilance of Intourist and other
organs of official Moscow slackens. I had packed his bag with
dozens of ballpoint pens, prized gifts for friends. The customs
man discovered one after another of the guilty little bundles,
tucked in corners, wrapped in handkerchiefs, until Henry soothed
his indignation with the bribe of a single openly offered Bic. It
was a happier customs experience than mine had been the
previous year. The young Intourist agent, busy on the phone
arranging a room in which to meet his girl, had misplaced
Henry's hotel assignment, so that, untypically, he was given a
choice of lodging. He elected the Metropole.

Arriving in the center of the city by taxi, he found the streets
hung with revolutionary banners, buildings lit up, carousers
everywhere, silhouettes reeling across the pink vision which is St.
Basil's. One word endlessly repeated on the banners, ВЛАСТЬ
("power"), in ALL POWER to the SOVIETS struck him as a loud
Pop Art declaration:

ВЛАСТЬ

ВЛАСТЬ

ВЛАСТЬ

ВЛАСТЬ

In front of the Metropole, four revelers were engaged in an
all-out drunken fistfight, each man for himself. The four women
in the party stood by, impassively watching as the men threw wild
haymakers and their bodies crashed back against parked Mosk-
viches. As Henry watched, a young militiaman approached the

fray. Gingerly, he tried to talk the combatants into behaving correctly—with little effect. Disorderly conduct was treated with leniency. Henry's mission, if discovered, would not be.

In his room, examining the worried plaster around light fixtures and switches, his first night-thoughts turned to the ill-fated Innokenty Volodin.

The next day he made his way through the grimly festive city, to different addresses, by foot and subway. In a short time a whole new world of friendships opened before Henry, who was in Moscow for the first time, yet he could let nothing interfere with the objective of his trip. On the second day, in a tiny apartment, in silence, he dashed off the prearranged sentences of our message to Solzhenitsyn and the diagrams on sheets of paper which were immediately read, memorized, and burned.

Awaiting the answers, he set forth on other encounters. It was considered far too dangerous at this time to attempt a direct meeting with Solzhenitsyn.

At the peak of the holiday he was driven to Peredelkino, despite the fact that it was by then off limits to foreigners, to visit Kornei Ivanovich Chukovsky.

Unfortunately, his escort brought him to the large, wooden, gingerbread house at the very moment of its master's afternoon nap. Henry's first glimpse of my friend was Chukovsky shouting from an upper window, "Go away! Go away!" He waved his arms wildly. Under no circumstances was he to be disturbed, by anyone, for any reason at all. How could the escort have been so foolish?

Later that afternoon, refreshed by sleep, Chukovsky with his female household entertained Henry and his sheepish companion at the four-o'clock main meal in a most expansive and genial manner. Afterward he led him, alone, to the upstairs studio where the photograph of me stood in the bookcase, the room where Solzhenitsyn had worked when he had stayed in the house. Chukovsky spoke of the rebirth of Russian literature, which was happening, he seemed to be saying, in this room, in Russia, in the world, with the advent of Alexander Solzhenitsyn.

Henry could not guess, any more than I had been able a year before, whether Chukovsky knew about our relationship with his former guest. What was certain was that, toward the end of his life, Chukovsky was gladdened by his own stand as a friend and benefactor of Solzhenitsyn.

Another of Henry's encounters was with Nadezhda Mandelstam. Along with Boris Pasternak, Osip Mandelstam was one of the greatest Russian poets of his generation. He had been caught in the Gulag net and in 1938, under uncertain circumstances, had died in a Siberian transit camp. After his death, his widow, Nadezhda (whose name means "hope"), remained as intensely devoted to his memory as she had been to the poet in his lifetime. She had managed to preserve his work through the Stalin years, in many cases committing entire poems to memory until they could be published abroad in the early 1960s.

In 1968, Nadezhda Mandelstam lived alone in Moscow, an almost legendary figure in the literary life of the city. Since my first visit to Russia, I had known her as a friend, a frail-looking, very feminine elderly Jewish woman of undiminished strength of mind and spirit. Now it was Henry's turn to meet her.

To avoid police-informer taxi drivers—always interested in the destinations of their foreign fares—he traveled to her address on the outskirts of the city by subway and a long walk. However, addresses in Moscow are not always simple. A single street number may apply to several adjacent apartment buildings, each a separate, unmarked "corpus" with equal claim to the mother address. By trial and error, using matches in the dark corridors, Henry eventually made his way to the right door in the right "corpus" and knocked. Nadezhda Mandelstam opened the door a crack. From her photographs he recognized her at once.

"I'm Henry," he told her in English (which she speaks fluently). "Olga's husband."

"Yes," she answered in a flat, lifeless voice. "What do you want?"

Henry understood. Years of awaiting the secret police, of knowing their ruses, had taught her to suspect every stranger.

"May I come in?"

"Of course." The same dead voice. No use to create a disturbance in the hallway.

In the plain little kitchen he showed her snapshots of me and our son.

"Very nice." No response. Anyone can carry family photographs.

Henry does not know what he said or did that convinced her that he was really who he said he was. Suddenly she was in his arms.

Over tea they talked the whole afternoon.

About Alexander Solzhenitsyn she said that he was a great man and a cunning man.

On the fourth day, walking slowly along the esplanade on the river side of the Kremlin, Henry was told Solzhenitsyn's replies to his message. Everything, it seemed, was understood. I was to act as his trustee in the case of *The Gulag Archipelago* exactly as I had done in that of *The First Circle*. We were to proceed with the new work as we had done with the first, with one exception: We were not to enter into a contract with Harper & Row until the translation was ready—in 1970 if possible—and we had signaled him by coded message that it was ready and had received his coded reply signifying "Proceed."

In the event of his arrest or death, however, we were to publish at once.

As for the ninety-six-chapter version of *The First Circle*, Solzhenitsyn agreed to keep this manuscript out of circulation in Russia and abroad.

He had also sent words of gratitude for our work on *The First Circle*.

The next day Henry left the Metropole under a pale winter predawn sky. On his floor, the "babushka" assigned to watch the comings and goings of tourists was sleeping, stretched out on three chairs pulled together. In the lobby, the Intourist hotel employees were nowhere to be seen. Outside, the bundled workers in trucks were taking down the propaganda banners.

No one questioned him at the airport. A sleepy search of his suitcase turned up nothing suspicious.

When his Swissair flight was airborne, he set to work transcribing from memory and from illegible squiggles in a notebook a score of messages, requests, words of friendship and love—words that all together said, "Do not forget us"—as well as the detailed instructions for the publication of *The Gulag Archipelago*.

14

WE WERE NEVER TO TASTE, even briefly, the satisfaction of the success of *The First Circle*. Nor could we breathe a sigh of relief that Solzhenitsyn, suddenly elevated to international celebrity, was any safer than before; on the contrary, the new manuscript now in our hands had raised the stakes in his contest with Soviet authorities. It was one thing for him to emerge cautiously as a dissident writer; quite another to appear boldly before the world, *in Russia*, as, in his own phrase, "another government."

These were exhilarating but difficult times for us. The flood of favorable reviews of *The First Circle* and *Cancer Ward* expressed the same passionate admiration we had been feeling for their prodigious author for a long time. We scarcely had time to skim over them. For by the time of publication in September 1968, we already faced constant decisions and tasks relating to the novel and to the new manuscript, which was slated to appear in two years. I remember thinking that we—with our secret organization based in the United States, and with others in Moscow, Paris, and elsewhere—were the body, the bones, muscles, and nerves, of an organism whose head was in the USSR. The body, receiving directions from the head, was enabling it to live. The head had, until now, caused the body to function in perfect accord with the head's purpose: survival in order to write. But now the whole organism was growing relentlessly in ways that no one could predict—no one except perhaps Alexander Solzhenitsyn himself.

During this time, the very success of *The First Circle* was creating problems for its author and ourselves. Since the June announcement, Harper & Row had been receiving inquiries about film rights and, when books became available, the inquiries became offers, ever more insistent. Since we had no definitive instructions about motion picture rights, we at first asked Alan Schwartz to respond by saying that no decision had been made, a tactic which only stirred greater interest. One offer, from a well-known European producer, was for a million dollars.

The problem we faced was a very unusual one, unique even in Alan's extensive experience with literary properties: how to say "no" to a million dollars with authority yet without revealing the source of that authority. We knew, from many discussions with Tony and Alan, that any production company would insist on knowing the basis of Harper & Row's copyright, soon unearthing the fact that the author had empowered someone living in the West to act as his trustee. Of course, such a disclosure at that time was out of the question. Besides, we felt that even if Solzhenitsyn should agree to a film, and even if the warranty question were safely resolved, the motion picture's quality and character would be impossible to control, and the novel might be turned into anti-Soviet propaganda or otherwise deformed. In any case, the publication of his novels was already bringing Solzhenitsyn the world renown that would favor his chances of pursuing his mission in the USSR. Publicity of the wrong kind, probing into the thickets of transmission of manuscripts and authorization, might harm him in official Soviet eyes. We continued to turn aside lucrative offers, awaiting the opportunity to obtain the author's instructions, but the tactic itself soon ran into trouble.

Harper & Row's refusal of all offers was beginning to attract attention.

From a film producer's standpoint, the publisher's apparent disdain for six- and seven-figure offers for the motion picture rights might well be a confession that the copyright stood on weak foundations. In that case, why not proceed—or threaten to proceed—with a film without buying the rights from the publisher?

We and Harper & Row faced such a threat, one which had to be contested lest the copyright of the work be endangered. Eventually we altered our strategy to meet it. We agreed with Alan that he should search out the producer-director team with the greatest potential of making a good film of *The First Circle*. Then we would be able to present a worthwhile proposal to Solzhenitsyn, thus holding off a pirated film, with its inevitable legal hazards. We had a number of meetings with Alan, sessions in which we turned from a policy of passive refusal to active search. Out of professional conscience, Alan advised us that very soon the standing offers would evaporate as the publicity surrounding the publication of Solzhenitsyn's novels died down, but he understood and sympathized with our reasons for not venturing into an area that would subject the copyright of *The First Circle* to scrutiny.

The resulting negotiations ultimately led to an agreement, though it was to take two years. These dealings were lengthy and required much skillful work by Alan, whose patience proved inexhaustible. The eventual argument for putting *The First Circle* into the chosen company's hands was that the director, Alexander Ford, an emigré moviemaker then living in Israel, had the approval of the author, a decisive fact we learned of through intermediaries.

SIX

The Italian Opera

15

THE YEAR 1968 had been marked by increasing repression in the USSR. The January trial of the dissidents Ginsburg and Galanskov, Brezhnèv's warning in March that intellectuals would be punished if they fell into "the net of Western ideologists," the military invasion of Czechoslovakia following the brief political springtime there—these were signs of the Soviet leadership's determination to crush any threat to the State's exclusive control of the minds of its citizenry. The Kremlin that year seemed filled with nostalgia for Stalin.

From Moscow, Henry had brought back two special requests made on Solzhenitsyn's behalf. The first was that a small tape recorder be purchased for him and delivered to an address in the vicinity of the capital. The other was Chukovsky's appeal that we take action to assure the observance of Solzhenitsyn's birthday.

On December 11, 1968, he would be fifty. Chukovsky told Henry that telegrams and letters of congratulation would be of importance in showing worldwide support for a writer in trouble with the State. In his own country, Solzhenitsyn was now a pariah. Angered and baffled by his campaign against censorship, the cultural officials were evidently divided over the question of how to deal with him. Everyone, however, understood that he was to be treated as a nonperson. It now took great courage to stand up for him.*

We telephoned and spoke in person to many friends about Solzhenitsyn's birthday. Others, in the United States and in Europe, were also spreading the word. On the eleventh, in the midst of our Connecticut birches and with Tom Whitney present, we drank toasts to Solzhenitsyn's health and to his survival.

Since Henry's return he had played the role of what we had come to call "the last person out of Russia," the returning visitor with the latest news from friends, the most recent messages and presents, and the freshest theories about the political convolutions within the USSR. A certain exaltation goes with this role, and Henry did not lack it. He was never to forget that visit. One evening he met people around a festive table in Moscow, on a memorable free-spirited occasion. That night, no one pointed to the ceiling. No one hesitated to meet him and speak freely to him. As nothing else had done so forcefully, it brought home to him the strength of that spirit of liberty and dignity which, wherever it does exist in Russia, stands against the forces of repression.

It was in this same spirit that we—and his audience in the West—honored Solzhenitsyn on his fiftieth birthday.

---

* One who did was Tvardovsky, the godfather of *One Day*. Another was Lydia Chukovskaya, Kornei Ivanovich's daughter. She was becoming the most eloquent spokesman for Alexander Solzhenitsyn in the USSR. Her open letters to Soviet literary officials, which circulated in *samizdat*, were giving a voice to the solidarity that persisted among the more courageous Soviet writers, like Chukovsky himself and Valentin Kaverin. Their support played a crucial part in his survival.

On that day, in the provincial town of Ryazan, hundreds of messages, from inside Russia and from abroad, flooded the post office, taking the officials by surprise.

Soon, the tape recorder would reach its destination.

I remember 1969 as being a year of hard work, of rumors and scares—the year during which a message that was at first incomprehensible reached us. As I look over our records of this period, I remember many sleepless nights. Rumors had begun circulating that somewhere in the West a publisher was about to bring out "Alexander Solzhenitsyn's latest book on Soviet concentration camps." In London, in New York, from Germany and Italy, such stories would surface, sometimes in the press, sometimes by word of mouth. Obviously, the existence of the "camp book" had been gleaned by individuals in the West and was now public information. Questions arose: Did the rumor of forthcoming publication apply to our group and Harper & Row: Or were one or more other publishers involved? Or was the rumor a fabrication that accidentally happened to be true?

We had Solzhenitsyn's assurance that there was no other copy in circulation—but what if something had gone wrong in the meantime? Perhaps there had been another "arrest" of his works by the KGB, perhaps they were deliberately circulating these in shadowy European intelligence circles in order to bring about a treason trial against him. Surely with such a book they would not dare—but how could we be certain?

At Solzhenitsyn's suggestion, first transmitted to us in January 1968, we had told Cass Canfield about our imminent possession of the new manuscript, about the publication plans that would go into effect on its author's signal. We believed that Harper & Row's interest in protecting their author's life coincided with their commercial interest in publishing his most important book, so that the secret would be kept.

As I look back on those rumors, I believe that some of them may have been based on statements made in America by Arkady Belinkov, a Soviet literary critic, once a labor camp inmate and one of Solzhenitsyn's 227 witnesses who provided material for

Gulag. Belinkov was the only person we were aware of at that time who knew about the existence of the "camp book." He had learned about it from Solzhenitsyn himself, before fleeing the USSR and settling in New Haven, Connecticut, where he resided until his death in 1970.

The rumors had a way of reaching Moscow with lightning speed. Time and again Solzhenitsyn would become persuaded that there were leaks somewhere within our organization, a terrifying prospect for him. He would rail against us and against Harper & Row, until in time, as opportunities arose, we would get word to him that *Gulag* and its secret were safe in our hands and that his instructions were being followed to the letter. Then, equally slowly—usually by the time a fresh crisis had arisen—he would return a message expressing gratitude and confidence.

Solzhenitsyn's alarm at the rumors about an unauthorized publication of *Gulag* was only one part of the story. The effect they had on our friends at Harper & Row—and indeed on the other members of our secret circle—was also devastating to us. At each report, we would receive phone calls and requests for meetings. Strong pressure was on us to signal the publication of *Gulag*. "It is already out in the open and we are obviously in a race." "Why lose time unnecessarily?" "Under the circumstances, to publish as soon as possible is in Solzhenitsyn's best interest." How often I heard these and half believed them.

These pressures created an oppressive climate for us, especially during the summer of 1969. By that time, Harrison Salisbury, whose good judgment we had always respected—and do to this day—and who acted as our senior counselor, had become convinced that *Gulag* had fallen into the hands of Western publishers other than Harper & Row.

With Tony and Alan we had already worked out the draft of a contract, so that whenever we received the signal we could sign it at once and proceed with publication. Now, in the face of the persuasive reports that others were rushing a translation to completion, Harrison was urging me to act. Tony too believed that delay would allow our unknown rivals to take the lead. Tom, with his enormous investment of work at stake, said nothing, but it was not difficult to sense his feelings. It was Harrison who spoke for the majority of our secret circle.

I remember particularly one call Harrison made. We were summering at Henry's family house on Nantucket. I was in his mother's bedroom. I could see myself vaguely in a darkened mirror—everything was deep blue, it was the end of a hot July day. Harrison's voice was insistent, his arguments a good deal more sharply edged than usual.

"Look here, Olga, are you sure you are doing Alexander Solzhenitsyn a favor by clinging to the letter rather than to the spirit of his trust? We must all put egotistic considerations aside. The man is in grave danger, the publication of *Gulag* may well save him at this time. What if the KGB was to outdistance you?"

In that peaceful room in the old brick house built by Quakers, the weight of the decision I faced was crushing.

What if Harrison was right? What if, under the circumstances, Solzhenitsyn wanted me to speed into print the edition of *Gulag* that would be his and not his enemies'?

Rather than confront those questions directly, I became angry. Another question arose in their place: Was Harrison treating me as an "unreasonable woman" who had to be talked into submission by strong masculine argument? I had already said that no matter what threats of a publishing race might arise we would follow Solzhenitsyn's last instructions to the letter. I and no one else was Solzhenitsyn's trustee for *The Gulag Archipelago* and I would not allow myself to forget it.

"The sooner *Gulag* appears the better it will be for Russia," said Harrison.

And indeed, all the arguments seemed to favor Harrison's position—except one: We had not received Solzhenitsyn's signal.

It was during that heated phone call that I abandoned all effort to reason out an answer to this question with so many unknowns. I fell back on the instinct that I had felt from the first.

"As long as Solzhenitsyn is alive and free," I told Harrison finally, "we will wait for his signal."

Looking back, I can better understand Harrison's position, which was a stronger one than I had realized. And it was shared by others. Solzhenitsyn himself, it now appears, was concerned about when *Gulag* should be published. He was deeply troubled by his own decision not to release it at once.

It was fortunate that I did not release *The Gulag Archipelago* that summer. On a beautiful, sun-flooded afternoon in late September, when the woods around our Connecticut house seemed to be on fire with unbelievable reds and oranges, I walked to our mailbox at the end of the long driveway and among the letters found a plain white envelope with a European postmark, no return address. Walking back to the house, I opened the envelope and read the unsigned message in French, typed on a small piece of onionskin paper. There were eight lines of instructions, most of which were clear enough: There were corrections of *Gulag*, which were to be picked up in Moscow; no foreign (other than American) publisher was to be approached until spring; certain photographs were to be included in *Gulag*. One of the instructions, however, I found bewildering.

Toutes les éditions en anglais, prévues et imprévues, doivent être autorisées, même sans paiement, à la seule condition qu'elles ne se prévalent pas d'un copyright puisqu'il y a lieu de favoriser YMCA.

I sat down on the grass under a tree and read that paragraph over and over. At first it would not yield to any key I could fit to it. If I was reading it correctly, it meant that almost everything we had undertaken for *Gulag*, on Solzhenitsyn's earlier instructions, would have to be undone.

One thing was clear. I was faced with another trip to Moscow. I thought with dread of the windowless room at Sheremetyevo airport, where I had been searched. Yet I would have to go to Moscow to pick up the corrections for *Gulag* and, above all, to try to unravel the meaning of that surprising paragraph in what we came to call the YMCA message.

All editions in English, foreseen and unforeseen, must be authorized, even without payment, on the one condition that they do not lay claim to a copyright, since there is reason to favor YMCA.

Was there *still* a failure of communication between us and Solzhenitsyn? Had he forgotten that he had asked us to promise *Gulag* to Harper & Row? He seemed to be saying that anyone had the right to publish an English-language edition and that all such editions would be viewed as "authorized" versions though none could hold copyright. That was reserved for the YMCA Press. But that was a contradiction in terms. If YMCA could not control the existence of other editions, the copyright was meaningless. Did Solzhenitsyn still not understand this?

Or had new pressures forced him to change his strategies, to seek new avenues for the dissemination of his books? Yet if this were true, why was he asking us to pick up the corrections for *Gulag* in Moscow?

I took the message to Henry. He read it over and for the first time since we had undertaken the Solzhenitsyn projects, he became angry.

"We can't do it that way," he said. "He mustn't go back on his agreement. He told us to promise it to Harper & Row. The fight over *Cancer Ward* was one thing, but a legal fight over *Gulag* and the secret will be out. They'll put him on trial for treason. We've got to persuade him to stick by the original agreement or, for his sake, get out altogether."

For hours, long into the evening, we debated the question, drifting further and further from a solution. Henry's words ". . . get out altogether" hung in the air.

For the first time we began to realize that we were not free to walk away from our involvement with the former *zek* in Ryazan. To resign when he needed us would be unthinkable—even though he might impose terms we believed would lead to catastrophe.

Once again, as soon as possible, I would have to try to go to Russia.

$$\overline{16}$$

IN THAT FALL of 1969, searching for a safe way to get to the USSR, I thought of my friend, the poet Robert Lowell.

For some time, Lowell had wanted to go to Russia. He had translated Mandelstam for my anthology, *Poets on Street Corners*, and had corresponded with Nadezhda Mandelstam, who admired those translations. He hoped to visit her in Moscow. There had been a plan that he, his friend Blair Clark, and Senator Eugene McCarthy travel together, with me accompanying them as an informal guide and interpreter. At first I had been indefinite. An American party which would include a distinguished poet and a prominent political figure was certain to be closely watched. On the other hand, no member of it was likely to be harassed. I had hesitated too because, as in the case of the Millers, I disliked traveling with friends under false pretenses, without letting them know of my involvement with Solzhenitsyn. But now that a visit was imperative, I decided to take Lowell up on his offer. Once again my feeling of uneasiness would be the price I paid for keeping Solzhenitsyn's secret. Of one thing I was certain: I would not travel to Russia alone, not after the episode at Sheremetyevo. I still dreamed of that windowless room at the airport, which resembled a setting out of *The First Circle*.

A few days after we received Solzhenitsyn's YMCA message, I telephoned Lowell at Harvard, where he was teaching one day a week, and told him that I was anxious to go to Russia as soon as possible and would be delighted to accompany him and his friends.

In early November, I went to New York to apply for a visa and to discuss the Russian trip with Lowell and Blair Clark. It was at that time, when I was staying with the Lowells at their New York apartment, that my host invited me to go with him to Washington, D.C., to participate in a large anti-war demonstration later that month.

Until then, my status as an alien and the demands of the Solzhenitsyn project had kept me from any political involvement. On impulse, I decided to go.

We arrived in Washington on an icy, sunny fall afternoon. The capital was already overflowing with marchers. Huge throngs of them, young and old, of every social and ethnic group, filled the airport. Within the city, more were arriving by car, bus, motorcycle, even by bicycle. This was still the sixties, and the costumes of the younger demonstrators had an Elizabethan richness— beards, long hair, earrings, tasseled jackets, high boots. Among the older participants. there were impeccably groomed WASPS and tweedy professors with elbow patches and massive horn-rimmed glasses. There were workers, businessmen, housewives, and hippies, people never seen together before, now gathered in Washington in opposition to the war.

At the hotel where we were to meet Blair, we ran into Norman Mailer and Dwight Macdonald. I was delighted when Lowell proposed that we go on the march together. Before setting forth into the crowded streets, we sat in Mailer's room over drinks. Macdonald and Lowell discussed Hertzen's memoirs and the contemporary Russian dissident movement. As I listened, I reflected on how much these Americans had come to understand about intellectual life in the USSR—and at the same time what a lag existed in that understanding because of their ignorance of *The Gulag Archipelago.*

Soon we set out into the autumn evening filled with demonstrators walking toward Arlington, where the march was to begin. Now the talk was about American politics. Macdonald, wearing a diminutive beret, was as dogmatic and engaging as ever, talking nonstop with erudition, charm, and the stubborn convictions of an old-fashioned radical, an American version of the elderly Russian revolutionaries I had known in childhood. Lowell, with his easy stride, still had the look of a young man, his graying hair closely cropped, the patrician visionary who would astound us with his striking insights into American destiny. Mailer, the pugilist, was in full control of his slugging intellectual incisiveness. All three were taking in the crowd, whose immensity was a source of pride to these early antiwar activists. Now and then passing students greeted them, usually recognizing Mailer first. Mailer would respond with a gruff, friendly word. All three delighted in the communion with the crowd. This is what political action could accomplish. This new, concerned America was their child.

I thought of three other men: Alexander Solzhenitsyn and his two campmates, the photograph of "the Three Musketeers."

I remembered other crowds: the masses of gray-faced Muscovites who every working day jam the sidewalks and subways of the capital, moving in slow, shuffling rivers.

I thought of Solzhenitsyn in the USSR working alone, in secret, readying the corrections of *Gulag*, trying to reach the conscience of a people locked in the grasp of its leaders, who were themselves imprisoned in lies and fear. President Nixon was said to be in the White House watching a football game on TV. The American government and the American people were dangerously out of touch. This march was a collective allegorical work called Vietnam, proclaiming that Americans would not follow the course of violence and destruction in which its leaders had been caught.

The marchers were carried along in a huge, warm wave of emotion. One lost the sense of one's body, one's ordinary preoccupations, becoming instead part of an immense, purposeful whole. It was getting dark and very cold as we stood on the bridge linking Arlington to the city. Below the bridge, on a grassy embankment, the headquarters of the march was established, a mass of tents and long makeshift tables. Each marcher was given a slip of paper with a number, the identification number of a GI killed in the war, and a candle to be sheltered inside a paper cup. We were to walk to the Capitol, four miles away, and deposit the numbered slips there, for delivery to the Senate the next day.

As we started moving very slowly across the bridge, traffic in the city came to a standstill. The march, which was to last well into the next day, with more marchers arriving during the night and into the morning hours, stretched as far ahead of us as we could see, an endless procession of people walking two or three abreast, carrying candles that flickered in the wind.

I remember the cold, which grew more penetrating as the evening wore on, and the immense avenues dotted with lights. For a long time the illuminated Capitol hung motionless in the night, refusing to grow bigger. Yet we did not tire, we only grew very cold. Dwight Macdonald, indefatigable and kindly, conversed steadily, sometimes stopping to chop the air with his hands to make a point. Mailer was at his most jovial, delighted to be recognized. Lowell, in contrast, talked intently about the dead in Vietnam, the Vietnamese and the Americans, their meaningless numbers. He recalled a poem by Mandelstam, which we had translated together. For me it evoked the world of *Gulag* as well:

> *Through the ether measured in decimals,*
> *light-time congeals to one beam,*
> *the numbers grow transparent with pain*
> *a mothlike summation of zeros.*

At this moment, the march and Solzhenitsyn's mission seemed to me a part of a single, proud enterprise.

The next day: more marches, more demonstrations. In the crisp, noon sun on the mall between the National Gallery and the Smithsonian, a mass of people so huge it was impossible to estimate its size had gathered in an orderly vigil. I had the feeling that the outsized architecture of Washington and the vast expanses of open space, scaled to the size of the country as a whole, were fulfilling their function now, receiving so many people in this solemn ceremony. At the National Gallery, young men and women in bohemian dress rested in the dark grandeur of the columned entrance hall at the top of the stairs. We four went in together for a look at the sumptuous lady from Petersburg, Titian's Venus, draped in fur and holding a mirror. In the late twenties, this painting had been sold by a Soviet government then in search of Western currency. Before that, it had been my father's favorite painting at the Hermitage.

Lowell was talking enthusiastically about going to Russia. We had to be sure to see the Rembrandts in Leningrad. We would spend as much time as possible visiting Nadezhda Mandelstam. As we spoke of Russia, I caught his spirit of optimism. What a relief it would be, I thought, to learn from Solzhenitsyn personally the full meaning of the YMCA message, to hear his latest plans for *Gulag*, to exchange information on a dozen pressing matters.

On the plane back to New York, filled with exhilaration from the impressions of the march, I made mental notes for the meeting I believed would soon take place in Moscow.

At that time I had no notion that Alexander Solzhenitsyn might view our steps along the freezing avenues of the American capital as a craven retreat from a just war, as a sign of the moral weakness of the West.

17

I RETURNED to Connecticut with renewed energies—and with a new feeling about becoming an American. For some time I had planned to be naturalized, but until now my intention was motivated solely by practical reasons. The march had awakened me to a new awareness of American experience. I looked forward to sharing the nationality of my husband and son and of those thousands I had felt at one with in the capital. But first the trip to Russia lay ahead.

That December we were working hard on the editing of *Gulag* Part One, with Tom pressing rapidly ahead with the translation of the entire work. Along with Christmas gifts, I collected medicines and other presents to bring to Russia. I wrote my Moscow acquaintances that I would be coming for a visit with Robert Lowell and a friend of his. Since Senator McCarthy had decided against going to the USSR at that time, the party was to include only three—Lowell, Blair Clark, and myself.

Henry, Tony, and I held conferences in New York to review Solzhenitsyn's situation as it stood following the YMCA message. As had we, Tony found this latest message both hard to grasp and ominous.

As the date of departure neared, I steeled myself for the trip, keeping my thoughts focused on the pleasure of seeing family and friends again.

Then, one January morning, less than a week before we were to leave, my travel agent called and in an astonished voice told me that Mr. Lowell's and Mr. Clark's visas had been issued by the Soviet consulate but mine had been denied. The agent had queried the Soviet embassy in Washington and learned that the refusal was categorical and not subject to appeal.

I remember at first feeling a sense of relief. I must have been more fearful of making the trip than I had known.

The possibility that I would be refused a visa had of course occurred to me, especially after the episode at Sheremetyevo. Even if the KGB had no clue to my relationship with Solzhenitsyn, I had traveled in the company of Arthur Miller, who at the time had been regarded by the Soviet authorities—quite wrongly—as an uncritical friend. Then *In Russia*, with Miller's text and Inge's photographs, was published. Saying much that is true about Soviet life, it is not uncritical. As the Millers' companion on part of the trip that produced that book, I was regarded as having contributed to Arthur Miller's disaffection with the USSR. It did not matter that this was an altogether absurd conception, that for many years he had followed the course of Soviet affairs with a keen and undazzled eye, that *In Russia* is the expression of a lifetime of thinking about the USSR.

The refusal might also have been linked to my poetry anthology. A full-page, virulent attack against it had been published not long before in the Writers Union paper, *Literaturnaya Gazeta*. It had been signed by one Pertzov, a minor literary figure said to have been among those who had hounded Mayakovsky just before his suicide. I knew that I had briefly become a celebrity in Moscow. Chukovsky had let me know that, at the time, an attack by Pertzov was regarded as the equivalent of a Pulitzer Prize.

I telephoned Lowell. Full of indignation on hearing the news about my visa, he decided on the spot not to go to Moscow. He said he would call Blair Clark.

When I hung up, the realization of what this refusal meant began to reach me. Blair Clark called. We talked a long time. He too would cancel his trip. He was troubled. He kept asking me *why* I had been refused entry. Did I have any idea? Wasn't it very unusual?

Sitting on my bed, looking out the window at the birches and the snowy meadow below our house, I realized I would not see my Russian friends for a long time. Perhaps never again. I was staring at the still trees and the snow, trying not to cry, trying not to let Blair Clark know how upset I was. As he hung up, my eye fell on the open suitcase on the floor in a corner of my room. It was ready to be closed, full of treasures—a warm robe for Nadezhda Mandelstam, baby clothes for the newborn Brodsky boy, a book by Salinger for Chukovsky. . . . I burst into tears.

Lowell's and Blair Clark's decisions not to go to Moscow without me left me even more desolate. I knew how much Nadezhda Mandelstam had been looking forward to Lowell's visit. She had already been told of our plans and would be bitterly disappointed.

And now we needed some other way to communicate with Solzhenitsyn. Another visit by Henry seemed unwise. We could not afford to establish any suspicious pattern. What we needed was a new messenger, someone trustworthy with no previous connection to Solzhenitsyn's affairs.

I remembered a friend in Paris, Marcel, a young man with a strong interest in Russian art who could also speak some Russian. I had not heard from him in years, but at one time we had seen each other often. He was reliable and well organized, yet also full of imagination. I wrote him a letter, asking him whether we could see him in Paris on a confidential matter of great importance, a "literary problem" that might make demands on his time. Marcel wrote back saying he was relatively free for the next few months and ready to meet us and hear what we had to say.

In the early spring we flew to Paris and spent long hours explaining to Marcel everything about our activities on behalf of Solzhenitsyn—including the situation created by the YMCA message. After much soul-searching, somewhat awed by the complexity and risks of the mission, he agreed to go to the USSR as soon as he could get a visa. Within a very few days, we saw him off at Orly, his suitcase loaded with Nadezhda Mandelstam's robe and the other presents I was not able to bring myself. We stayed in Paris, working on the editing of *Gulag*, praying that nothing would go wrong in Moscow that might bring Solzhenitsyn—and our messenger—into the grasp of the Archipelago.

In a few days we were again at Orly, waiting for the return of our emissary. I remember, amid the subdued Parisian spring light, entering the terminal and scanning the arriving passengers. I remember, too, our sense of relief when we spotted Marcel's youthful figure atop the central escalator.

There were bear hugs and greetings, and we knew at once from his exuberance that he had been successful in his mission. I remembered my own first meeting with Solzhenitsyn. In Marcel's eyes I thought I saw a reflection of his presence.

"He sends you both his warmest greetings," he announced, aware of our intense curiosity about what had passed between them. "And to your friends in America."

"He's well?" I asked.

"Extremely. Full of new plans, ideas—facing an extraordinarily difficult situation brilliantly. A splendid man—a giant of a man —a deeply religious man!"

Our silence asked the question in both our minds. We had had indications that the Orthodox Church was of importance to Solzhenitsyn, but we were surprised that his religious nature was one of Marcel's stronger impressions of him.

"Oh, yes," he insisted, "deeply religious."

"And his new plans?" asked Henry.

Marcel looked from one to the other of us. He seemed suddenly wary; then with a laugh he said he must catch his breath before telling us more, since there was indeed much to tell—"All fascinating, fascinating! What an astonishing man!" On the way to our car, Marcel diverted us with stories of his Moscow experiences. Then we drove to his apartment and heard the rest of Solzhenitsyn's message.

The first thing he told us was that the publication of *The Gulag Archipelago* was to be delayed for a long time.

Hearing this, I felt tremendous relief. The responsibility for a project I believed was likely to doom its author was suddenly lifted. Thank God, I thought, we had made no formal commitment to Harper & Row.

As for the English translation, it was to be completed and held until its eventual publication. Solzhenitsyn was now at work on another project, an epic multivolume novel about World War I and the Russian Revolution. His decision to suspend *Gulag* had evidently been made in part to give him time to finish that work, which he had come to regard as the principal literary endeavor of his life.

According to Marcel, all aspects of Solzhenitsyn's life were in turmoil. It was a time of shaking off the bonds of the past and opening new avenues for the pursuit of his goal, now altered from a desperate, possibly terminal act of publishing the truth about the prison camp system to a historic novel about the birthpangs of the Soviet state which had produced the camp system.

As we listened in wonderment, Marcel described the new arrangements under which the dissemination and control of Solzhenitsyn's literary works abroad would from now on take place.

Solzhenitsyn had engaged a Swiss lawyer to represent him in the West, Dr. Fritz Heeb. He had authorized Heeb to look after his interests openly and publicly, to sign contracts for future books and to supervise the quality of all translations of his works. However, our ward, *The Gulag Archipelago*, was to remain in our hands. It was to be kept entirely outside of Dr. Heeb's sphere of activity. It is possible that Dr. Heeb was not even informed of the existence of *Gulag* at that time. In any case, we were to proceed as before with the editing in Russian and with completing the translation into English, then preserve it in the deepest secrecy.

Who was this Dr. Heeb? we asked.

All Marcel could tell us was that he was said to belong to a Social Democratic Zurich family, that he had been a Communist but had left the party some years before, possibly on a matter of principle. All was mysterious, indefinite. How had Solzhenitsyn chosen him? We were even uncertain how to pronounce his name.

Dr. Heeb (the pronunciation turned out to be Heb) was, however, only a part of the new arrangement.

The third item in Marcel's message from Solzhenitsyn was the hardest to grasp. Marcel drew a diagram to explain it. As he did so, I had the feeling that he was savoring the mysteries Solzhenitsyn had created.

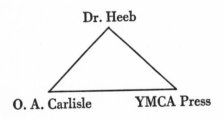

Dr. Heeb

O. A. Carlisle   YMCA Press

This was the "triangle of authority" through which Solzhenitsyn would secretly act in the West. His works would be managed by a three-cornered administration, composed of Dr. Heeb, his official legal representative; YMCA Press, a well-known Russian-language publisher; and myself, the secret trustee and custodian of *The Gulag Archipelago*.

Each of the three members was to fulfill his assigned role, with Dr. Heeb responsible for the open representation of his client's interests (other than *The Gulag Archipelago*) and Marcel serving as a messenger between us and the YMCA Press in Paris.

Though diffident about his own role in this network, Marcel was anxious to see Solzhenitsyn's new arrangements and ours fit together.

On that day we did out best to share his confidence that the triangle could work efficiently. We respected Solzhenitsyn's wish to shift the center of operations from the United States to Europe. We could understand that he might feel he had given us too much power over his fortunes and now intended to divide his new empire into satrapies, each watchful of the other, with checks and balances and emissaries, all competitive in their obedience to the distant authority. Through Marcel we thought we could detect Solzhenitsyn's zest in setting up his personal bureaucracy abroad, with splendidly Byzantine ins and outs.

As Marcel explained these directives, we tried to grasp exactly what Solzhenitsyn intended and how we could adapt ourselves to the new situation. We had other meetings with Marcel, whose responsiveness to Solzhenitsyn was ardent. He had gone to Moscow as our emissary and returned as ours and as Solzhenitsyn's as well. He was doing a very difficult job well. Solzhenitsyn's instructions, though complex, were categorical. Marcel did his best to present them as Solzhenitsyn himself would have done, though he shared our fear that the new arrangements would expose the secret of our activities.

On the plane to New York my feelings caught up with me. I felt drained and apprehensive. I could see danger ahead in a triumvirate that was to straddle the Atlantic. Henry shared these feelings. He took out his notebook and studied the triangle again.

"Looks like a cabalistic sign," he said. After a moment he added, "The worst is, he's not listening anymore."

18

As I write these words, Alexander Solzhenitsyn is alive and well. He lives in closely guarded seclusion in Vermont, at work on his writing and embarked on a nonprofit publishing venture. Between 1970 and 1974, when he was expelled from the USSR, our involvement with him took many intricate turns, acquiring a bizarre character very different from that of the first three years we had devoted to his publishing affairs.

Until 1974, when Solzhenitsyn stepped off the plane in Frankfurt, every action of ours had still to be weighed against its probable effect on his survival. Through all that time, I had the feeling of running just to stay in place. Success was measured in terms of averting disaster. But there was also satisfaction in watching the Russian human rights movement gain international sympathy and support. There were also moments of diverting relief.

On one of my many trips to Europe for meetings with the emissaries who had become part of Solzhenitsyn's enlarged network abroad, I decided to escape for a weekend in my favorite Italian city, Venice. Our son, who was then living in Paris, joined me there. One evening we went to the opera at the Fenice. This eighteenth-century theater, with its evocations of Casanova, is as charming as the city that is its home. The opera was Donizetti's *Cardinale de Rohan*. Despite a childhood steeped in Dumas's historical romances, I found myself bewildered by the story from beginning to end. Characters would appear on stage and sing arias, spirited or lugubrious, then disappear. A monk serenading a skull cradled in his hands was suddenly replaced by a swarm of musketeers in lace collars, brandishing oversized muskets and singing a rousing military tune.

After a while, the bellicose musketeers gave ground to the cardinal, remonstrating with a fat woman. Though she was enormous, her diaphanous costume identified her as the ingenue. Suddenly she cast herself to the floor, skirts flying over her head, and attempted to stab herself with a dagger. As the opera proceeded to its finale, each scene became more perplexing. At last, the heavy damask curtains closed, then opened again to reveal the cardinal and the restored ingenue bowing to a standing ovation.

Today, with Solzhenitsyn out of the USSR, I look back on the period of our involvement with him between 1970 and early 1974 as the Era of the Italian Opera. At the time, given what was at stake, it was harrowing. We were then part of the enlarged cast, with many continuing responsibilities and diminishing authority to fulfill them. The cardinal might remonstrate, yet he remained as vulnerable as ever. If anyone made a false step, the cardinal might die. We felt that we were being drawn into a world of intrigue, a world in which we began to feel like conspiratorial agents, uneasy about our roles but unable to step out of them.

When Henry and I returned to the United States after Marcel's briefing, we had meetings with Tony and with Alan Schwartz about the new instructions. At this time, we received a report that a European publisher was claiming possession of *The Gulag Archipelago*. We were alarmed. Alan set about to check on this news and ascertained that it was unfounded. In a Paris café, Marcel met with a woman now involved in the triangle, a woman I shall call Eva. She was a friend of Dr. Heeb's. As to the question of Eva's knowledge of our identities, Marcel appears to have conducted himself with elaborate circumspection. He wrote, "At one point, she said 'them.' I did not respond at all, any more than I'd have done had she said 'she' or 'he.' But she said 'them.' " Eva, apparently, knew much. She was in Solzhenitsyn's confidence. We had no instruction to make direct contact with her or with Dr. Heeb. The triangle was not to go into operation till summertime.

Meanwhile, on Solzhenitsyn's request, we were investigating the character of another young man in Paris, who was also to play a key role in the three-cornered organization. I shall call him Boris. After making inquiries of friends who knew him well, we were able to recommend Boris for the role Solzhenitsyn had provisionally assigned him, that of his Russian-language editor abroad.

At this time, early spring 1970, Cass Canfield decided to undertake direct shuttle diplomacy with Dr. Heeb. We objected sharply: Such a meeting was premature. *The Gulag Archipelago* was in our charge under the condition that it be discussed with no one. Dr. Heeb's province was to handle all matters that could be dealt with openly. If Cass entered into talks about *The Gulag Archipelago* with Dr. Heeb he would almost certainly turn the author against his firm and against us. Harper & Row was now the presumptive publisher of this work, whenever the time came to release it. Additional pressures could only be destructive. Cass canceled the trip.

In April, Dr. Heeb's role as Solzhenitsyn's legal representative was announced in Europe and the United States. Solzhenitsyn's unprecedented act of allowing it to be publicly known that he had hired a western legal representative caused intense commotion. For the first time, a Soviet writer had come above ground in his dealings with the West. Outside the USSR, there was shock and fear for his safety in the days immediately following Heeb's announcement. Inside the Soviet Union, there was consternation. And yet, something kept the Soviet authorities from acting against Solzhenitsyn.

In his public statement, Dr. Heeb warned that any future publication of the author's work could take place only under contractual authorization by the writer "or his legal representative." And, in the story in the *London Times*, there appeared the following: "Now it is reported that another of his main works, *Arkhipelag Gulag*, meaning literally Labour Camp Archipelago, and dealing with Stalinist concentration camps, is being offered for sale in Europe and America."

The rumor Alan had only shortly before checked out and found false had not yet been laid to rest.

Soon, from Moscow (via couriers) we received frantic messages of alarm. A typical one was the following:

Dear Friend,

We are well, but the springtime is unusually warm. Everyone suffers from the heat.

We are deeply disturbed to learn that the doctor's advice has not been followed and that travel has been permitted to various countries.

Complete rest is essential now. How can this be misunderstood? Sergei's life depends on it.

We hope you will enjoy the forthcoming concert, beginning with the Tchaikovsky. Please do not miss it.

Also, please do not send size 7½ gloves.

With all good wishes

Approximate translation:

Dear Friend,

We are alive but everyone is closely watched.

We are deeply disturbed that *The Gulag Archipelago* ms. has been allowed to reach foreign publishers.

The ms. must be shown to no one now.

We expect you to be involved in the "triangle," as directed, beginning with the meeting with Eva.

Do not deal with [a certain film company] in connection with film rights to *The First Circle*.

With all good wishes

Receiving such a message, we had to cast about for a safe means of making assurances to those in Moscow—for example, that no manuscript of *The Gulag Archipelago* had in fact been released to any publisher. Usually, an opportunity was not long in coming.

In one instance in late spring, we were fortunate that friends of ours met with Solzhenitsyn and his new wife for a picnic in a clearing in a Russian forest. It had rained earlier that day and the encounter began badly. Solzhenitsyn, wearing his camp jacket, sat on the ground, his brow furrowed, poring over a copy of *The First Circle*.

"An outrage!" he was saying. "My work hopelessly garbled. Look at this!"

And he pointed to some offending line.

Our friends were dismayed. They were close to us; they knew how hard we had worked, and under what difficult conditions, to assure that such errors would not appear. They spoke of what a great success *The First Circle* had been, but to little avail. Solzhenitsyn would soften a little, then come upon another abomination that would send him into a fury.

Gently, asking his permission, one of our friends took the book from his hands. She opened it to the title page and read the name of the publisher.

"Alexander Issayevich," she said quietly. "This is not the edition they were responsible for. This is the pirated edition that caused such a commotion when it came out in Europe. It was said to be financed by the KGB and has since been stopped."

Solzhenitsyn took back the book, staring at it in astonishment; then he tossed it aside.

"Friends, friends, we must trust each other," he said at last. "Above everything else, we must trust each other."

Our friends swear that at that moment the skies began to clear.

The rest of that encounter passed in an atmosphere of warm friendship, with repeated pledges of mutual confidence and trust. Solzhenitsyn gallantly removed his camp jacket and spread it on the damp ground for our friend who had had the correct hunch about the pirated edition.

At this meeting Solzhenitsyn stressed again that he wanted to postpone the publication of *The Gulag Archipelago*. He acknowledged that he had been hasty in bidding us to inform Harper & Row about its existence and to say that it would eventually be published by them. Our friends assured him that, despite the rumors, no copy made from our microfilm existed at Harper & Row or at any other publisher and that existing photostats were carefully guarded by Tom and ourselves. They assured him that if a manuscript did surface anywhere else it would have to have come from another source. Solzhenitsyn was greatly relieved. He in turn assured our friends that no other microfilm of *The Gulag Archipelago* had left the USSR.

As for Dr. Heeb, Solzhenitsyn said that he was to have nothing to do with the publication of either *The First Circle* or *The Gulag Archipelago*. We were to proceed with the translation of the latter work in the greatest secrecy. For other future publications, Dr. Heeb would handle world rights except that we would be responsible for English-language territories. Russian-language editions would be YMCA's province.

The forest meeting ended on a note of exaltation. Dr. Heeb, Eva, Boris, Marcel, our friends from the forest meeting, and ourselves were to work as a coordinated task force, some in secret, Dr. Heeb in the open. The Italian Opera had been cast.

After leaving Russia, the participants of the forest gathering met in Western Europe with Eva and, at her suggestion, with Dr. Heeb. More pledges of goodwill, dedication, and cooperation were exchanged. Still, questions of how the new plan would work in practice, without overlapping authority, leaks, and failures of communication, loomed larger than ever.

By summer 1970, while Alan was concluding the delicate negotiations to forestall new threats of a pirated film of *The First Circle*, Cass Canfield received a letter from Dr. Heeb saying in part, "I am very anxious to beg you *not* to sell motion picture rights . . . concerning *The First Circle*." Consternation. Since Solzhenitsyn had assured us that his legal representative would have no say in matters relating to *The First Circle*, the message increased our misgivings about the triangle.

We decided to meet with Dr. Heeb.

19

In early August 1970, Tony and I went to Switzerland to meet Dr. Heeb. We had by then verified that, though the two had never met, the Swiss lawyer was in fact empowered to act for Solzhenitsyn in the West. That spring, Tony had entered into correspondence with the new representative and had decided that constructive working relations could be established between him and ourselves.

As we arrived in Switzerland, we were full of curiosity about the man we were to meet. In Tony's briefcase was an agenda for the encounter. We hoped to establish a clear agreement on our respective functions and powers.

There would soon be a small distribution of funds to Dr. Heeb pending a transfer to him of the accumulated royalties of *The First Circle*. In addition, we were to share with him the wishes Solzhenitsyn had expressed to us about the use of his money in the event of his death: first, to build a church near Leningrad; second, to restore the Solovki Monastery; third, to finance a periodical devoted to Russian literary criticism and political thought.

Tony was hopeful that these and other matters could be resolved smoothly. I believe that the prospect of transferring to Dr. Heeb the eventual responsibility for building a church and restoring a monastery in the Soviet Union put Tony in a cheerful mood.

On the warm summer morning before our meeting, Tony went sailing. By noon, the hour of the meeting, he was in love with Switzerland and with the sunny town on the blue lake where the encounter was to take place. His roundish, suntanned face radiated goodwill and positive thinking. Though I had traveled alone and extensively on Solzhenitsyn's business, I was very glad that Tony was with me on this trip.

Outside the windows of the apartment where we met, the streets were festive, filled with tourists enjoying a summer holiday. Inside, as the American lawyer and the Swiss lawyer shook hands, I was struck by the contrast between the two. Dr. Heeb was in his fifties, tall, with short, graying hair and a squarish face. Everything about him in fact, even the cut of his brown suit, suggested right angles. Tony, shorter, almost two decades younger, was all roundness and bounce.

Self-conscious about his English, Dr. Heeb retreated behind walls of matter-of-factness and stiff civility. Conversation faltered. Tony rescued it by finding that Dr. Heeb was interested in the outdoors. Over coffee we talked about the beauty of the Swiss mountains and the pleasures they afforded. Hiking in the summer. Skiing in the winter. Then, following a lengthy pause, Dr. Heeb spoke of "our friend" and, in carefully chosen, reverent words, of the honor it was to serve him. I could detect, however, no feeling of *shared* dedication behind his immobile façade. He was so very guarded with the Americans who had worked for his new client. I suspected that he found our candid, friendly behavior inappropriate to the situation. Nor in my case did our common socialist background create any bond between us. And the shared admiration of mountains was not enough.

I began to doubt whether the meeting of minds Tony had predicted was at hand.

Soon, as Tony and I had agreed beforehand, I left the lawyers to discuss the business at hand privately. The door had not shut behind me before Tony was snapping open his briefcase with an air of getting down to work under the most promising of conditions.

That hot afternoon I went to the beach to swim. A troubling thought had occurred to me. At our second encounter, Solzhenitsyn had vigorously denounced the Socialist Revolutionaries— knowing that I was a descendant of a prominent SR. Now, in appointing Dr. Heeb, he had chosen another socialist, an ex-Marxist in this case, to act as his representative in the West. Solzhenitsyn had indicted Socialist Revolutionaries only for their incapacity to sustain action; his rejection of Marxism and Marxists, however, was total.

Why, then, would he create a triangle of which two of the elements were, in his eyes, flawed? And those two elements were, moreover, traditionally at odds with each other.

All that summer afternoon I could not shake off this thought.

At four, Tony and I met for tea. He pronounced the meeting with Dr. Heeb a complete success.

20

In October 1970, Alexander Solzhenitsyn was awarded the Nobel Prize for Literature. Again, champagne flowed in Connecticut. This honor greatly strengthened Solzhenitsyn's hand in the Soviet Union. It was one thing for the KGB to pound on the door of a dissident writer and drag him off into the night, quite another to arrest a Nobel laureate.

Solzhenitsyn had long been aware of what winning the prize could mean to his strategies. I thought back to a walk I had taken one day in the early spring of 1967, right after my first encounter with him. A friend of his, a warm-hearted, generous man who had shared his prison camp experiences (and who knew nothing of what had passed between us), invited me out for a stroll, away from his bugged apartment. As we walked along the Sadovy Circle, still leafless and wintery-looking, he told me insistently,

"Alexander Issayevich must have the Nobel prize. It is extremely important. Olga Vadimovna, consider this! You must do everything possible to bring it about."

Solzhenitsyn's friend, tall, burly, full of life, did not bother to lower his voice as he spoke. His eyes were fiery and he waved his fur hat in the air, punctuating his words with it. At the time, I was touched by his enthusiasm. I remember telling him that he was greatly overestimating my potential influence in Western literary circles. I thought to myself that with only *One Day* published, Solzhenitsyn was not likely to be considered for a Nobel prize, at least not for many years. Yet now, only three years later, following the publication of *The First Circle* and *Cancer Ward*, he had become the fourth Russian, after Bunin, Pasternak, and Sholokhov, to receive the award.

Beyond contributions to the publication of *The First Circle* and behind-the-scenes promotion of its author, I had done nothing directly to help Solzhenitsyn along the road to Stockholm. Nevertheless I felt a sense of accomplishment that day—a feeling that stood forth in relief against the mounting frustration we were then experiencing in trying to work productively within the triangle.

By this time, Harper & Row was in direct negotiation with Dr. Heeb. They were beginning to sound him out on eventual publication of future novels. Messages were flying between the European corners of the triangle. Rumors about Solzhenitsyn and the publication of his new works crackled in one European capital after another: He was about to be condemned in Russia as an agent of Zionism; *The Gulag Archipelago* was about to come out in Italy; in Paris, a young woman was claiming to be his representative. We could ignore no report, no matter how farfetched, in charting our own course.

Meanwhile, in Moscow, Solzhenitsyn himself was engaged in a contest with the Swedish authorities. The Swedes were at pains not to allow him to use their embassy in Moscow as an arena in which the writer, as "a second government," would pit himself against the existing one. When Solzhenitsyn decided not to go to

Sweden to accept the Nobel prize, proposing instead that it be awarded at a ceremony in the embassy. Swedish officials, fearing trouble with the USSR, demurred; talks ensued.

During that winter of 1970–71, Henry and I, with Tony's help, were working out a plan for our partial disengagement from Solzhenitsyn's affairs—a disengagement that would reflect the de facto situation created from Moscow by Solzhenitsyn himself. The plan was that we would be responsible for *The Gulag Archipelago* and leave everything else to Dr. Heeb, including publishing arrangements in the United States and England for all other books. I would end my trusteeship of *The First Circle* and decline any involvement with *August, 1914*, the first volume of Solzhenitsyn's panoramic work about the Russian Revolution. Our rationale was that, with *The First Circle* successfully published, our task had been accomplished and our present work should be limited to the custodianship and eventual worldwide publication of *The Gulag Archipelago*. On March 4, 1971, a letter was sent to Dr. Heeb setting forth this new proposal.

What seemed both right to us and responsive to Solzhenitsyn's wishes, however, was not to appear so in the swirling fogs of the triangle.

That same March, a show of my paintings was opening in Paris. I traveled to Europe to help set it up—but also to engage in conversations with Dr. Heeb, Marcel, Boris, and our friends from the picnic meeting in the forest. I found myself in a surreal world.

Eva, whom I had yet to meet, and our friends were in touch with each other, discussing how Solzhenitsyn's directives were to be carried out. Boris, who had no concern for Harper & Row's contractual interests in *The First Circle*, had to be told why he should consider their position before publishing the ninety-six chapter version of the novel, which had been sent to him by Solzhenitsyn. It appeared that, for Solzhenitsyn, it was now of paramount importance that this version be shared with the widest public possible. Earlier, he had had to tamper with his conception of *The First Circle* in the hope that it would eventually be published in the Soviet Union. Thus, for instance, he had made the information passed on by Volodin medical in nature when, in fact, it had been an atomic secret. Now he wanted an authentic version of his masterwork made known to the world.

It was then that I learned that, unknown to ourselves or to Dr. Heeb, the manuscript of *August, 1914* had been given to YMCA Press in Paris for an immediate surprise publication in Russian. As for Dr. Heeb, the question uppermost in his mind appeared to be: Was it obligatory to offer to Harper & Row the American rights to Solzhenitsyn's future books? My answer: not at all, but everything considered—including their successful experience with *The First Circle*—it might be a sensible idea.

I had the feeling at this period that some of our European correspondents would not be displeased if some sort of unholy bonds were discovered linking us with Harper & Row in a capitalist plot aimed at subverting the selfless motives of a great dissident writer. I began to sense a growing climate of mistrust on the part of our European contacts toward both the American secret circle and the American publisher.

While Paris hummed with talk of Solzhenitsyn and his clouded future, I felt as if I were turning into a cybernetic machine, a Solzhenitsyn computer. As I supervised the hanging of my paintings at the gallery on the Quai de Conti, I wondered when I would be able to return to my painting—and to a free life—again.

ON APRIL 1, Dr. Heeb wrote Tony in reply to our letter of March 4: "Now as before you and your client have the charge of K2 [*The Gulag Archipelago*] on the basic [sic] of the instructions of our friend."* In the same letter, he also agreed to the limitation of our role to this one work.

I returned to Connecticut utterly exhausted from the trip but

_____

* In our code, *The First Circle* was K1, *Gulag* was K2, and *August, 1914* was K3.

with the feeling that perhaps, after all, I had accomplished something toward keeping lines of communication open.

"We must all do our human best," a friend close to Solzhenitsyn had said. I agreed wholeheartedly.

But in July 1971, fresh signs of confusion appeared.

Without further consultation with us, Dr. Heeb offered *August, 1914* not to Harper & Row but to Farrar, Straus & Giroux. This was of course Dr. Heeb's prerogative, and the firm he had chosen was an excellent one. But in the letter informing us of this decision, he let fall hints that the fortunes of *The Gulag Archipelago* were also to be directed via Zurich, despite all that had been so recently confirmed to the contrary.

The rest of 1971 passed in continuing negotations between ourselves and Dr. Heeb about our divided responsibility. At this time, substantial sums were still being held in trust for Solzhenitsyn. Then in January 1972, Tony and I went to Zurich to conclude all business between us and Dr. Heeb. Our accounting was presented for approval. It provided for payment of the balance of Solzhenitsyn's earnings from *The First Circle*, less reserves for final expenses relating to *The Gulag Archipelago* and a sum placed in escrow in the event of legal liabilities.

During the spring and summer of 1972, signals reached us from all quarters indicating that the "era of good feelings," exemplified by Solzhenitsyn's generous acknowledgment of our services, was at an end. From Eva, from Marcel, from persons in Moscow, a jumble of reports was forming into one increasingly plain message: Solzhenitsyn was displeased. He was displeased with the translations of his works.* And he felt that we were favoring Harper & Row's publishing interests over his own. The

---

* At this time, the Michael Glenny translation of *August, 1914* was under attack by reviewers. Glenny was to reply with a heartfelt defense, citing the lack of opportunity he was given to bring the work to completion. Dr. Heeb's first excursion into the English-language domain was conspicuously unsuccessful in the area that seemed to matter most to Solzhenitsyn—translation.

spirit of the forest meeting ("Above everything else, we must trust each other") seemed dead.

In the late summer of 1972, I went to Europe to confer with others involved in the triangle and to try to penetrate the mists. At a café, I met Eva for the first time. From the start, she spoke as Solzhenitsyn's emissary with instructions for me; yet it was impossible to sort out which injunctions were her own, which Dr. Heeb's, and which Solzhenitsyn's.

". . . and the lawyer you have," she told me. "With Dr. Heeb representing Alexander Issayevich, he isn't needed now. And he's so expensive. I do think that our friend would be gratified if, as a gesture of goodwill toward him, you would fire Mr. Curto."

She so surprised me with what seemed a high-handed intrusion into our affairs that I broke my rule against entering into dispute and explained that Tony Curto was indeed still needed, and was, besides, drawing at this time only reduced fees. There was no question of dismissing him.

"But you understand," Eva went on, "from now on *all contracts will be signed by Dr. Heeb. It must be that way. In this I completely agree with Alexander Issayevich.*"

This time I kept silent. Here was a confirmation of what had so far only been hinted at: Solzhenitsyn intended that Dr. Heeb would take control of *The Gulag Archipelago* after all, while we would remain responsible only for its publication in the United States. World rights no longer, it seemed, would be handled by Harper & Row.

Eva then suggested that we put our heads together to set up a committee to select a French translator for *Gulag*, a subject about which I found it difficult to be enthusiastic. In 1970, after I had found a highly competent and trustworthy person to translate this book into French, Solzhenitsyn had ordered the work stopped. This was at a time when he was postponing the publication of *Gulag* indefinitely.

"Of course, you would be a member of the translation committee," Eva said. "That goes without saying. Along with myself and three or four other trusted experts."

I REMEMBER the afternoon flight home, the feeling of timelessness as I moved westward with the sun. I now had reason to hope that Dr. Heeb would be taking full charge of his client's affairs. In effect, Solzhenitsyn himself was releasing me from what had become a bondage.

For the first time in years I surveyed what my connection with him was doing to my life. I was separated forever from my Russian relatives and friends; my career as a journalist specializing in Soviet affairs seemed permanently compromised; the possibility of devoting myself fully to painting was still far in the future, since the business of disengaging ourselves from the involvement would be long and laborious. As for Henry, though he continued to spend as much time as was necessary on Solzhenitsyn's problems, he was becoming increasingly frustrated by the turn they were taking. His patience was wearing thin. What had been a creative publishing adventure, one which had brought us closer together, was becoming an exercise in futility. He was now at work on a new novel but still had to participate in these never-ending, ever-crumbling charades. Russian charades, for which I couldn't help but feel responsible.

In the endless midafternoon over the Atlantic, I was suddenly seized with deep sorrow. I was overwhelmed by the magnitude of the responsibility I had assumed, by what for the first time I recognized clearly as Solzhenitsyn's repudiation.

I tried to fight back my depression. At least, I reflected, I was returning to the United States with enough information to permit Henry and me to see where matters stood and to make a decision.

Soon afterward, I wrote a letter destined for Solzhenitsyn. I let him know that either I would carry out my obligations under the original arrangement, as his trustee, holding *The Gulag Archipelago* until his signal, then concluding arrangements for worldwide publication, or we would turn over all authority and responsibility to Dr. Heeb.

Quite aware that such a message was likely to aggravate Solzhenitsyn's displeasure, we could nonetheless find no alternative.

We settled in for the winter, awaiting Solzhenitsyn's reply.

SEVEN

Into the Fire

21

In January 1973, I traveled once again to Paris, this time solely to visit with members of my family, including an uncle and an aunt I had not seen for several years. For the first time since 1967 I felt that I was traveling on my own, not on urgent business for Solzhenitsyn; yet not long after I greeted my family, it became clear that I was to be drawn deeper than ever into the Italian Opera.

Letters from Eva kept arriving. One, translated from the writer's Russian, gives some idea of the style—and the content— of all of them. In it, she is deliberating on how to choose a French translation for *Gulag*.

We must be sure of one thing—and I ask you to reflect on this. In order to find a modus for the "verification" of the translator it is unthinkable to give a thousand and more pages at risk: what might the result be? Yet this happens; even with experienced ones it does not work out, as much did not work out in *August*, though the brigade of translators had proved itself earlier—and well. I have this vision, let's say, on the pretext of the next "knot," to commission several people for a trial translation, for example, a few pages out of the Nobel prize speech (a difficult enough text), then it would be checked out and approved by two or three specialists, including you, of course, but not colleague-translators. This would be most convenient to conduct in the name of [Boris] as A.I.'s publisher, but since you do not want this it can also be done in the name of our Zurich doctor.

At this time I still had no answer from Solzhenitsyn to my proposal to manage that book exclusively, as previously agreed, or to resign responsibility to "our Zurich doctor." Since Eva was then planning a trip to Moscow, I wrote her, restating our position, asking that Solzhenitsyn make a choice.

Eva wrote back that she *had* in fact received an answer from Solzhenitsyn to our letter concerning the administration of *Gulag*. The matter had not seemed to her of sufficient urgency to pass on in her letters at this time. She did not wish to disrupt the functioning of the triangle with what she took to be legalistic irrelevancies. The present status of *Gulag*, she wrote, was as follows:

1. [We were] to discuss collectively the question of the French translation.
2. All agreements from now on are to be signed solely by Dr. Heeb (in this I am completely in agreement with A.I., nothing else would be possible)....
3. Harper & Row are given rights for their own country.
4. You have, obviously, the rights for the English language. It seems to me that in this matter of rights (their extension into England or South America*) you may write and possibly

---

* "My God," said Henry when later I read him this letter, "she thinks they speak English in South America."

come to an agreement with A.I. directly. This does not seem to me so much a question of principle. The principle here is that the legal arrangements are to be handled by Dr. Heeb. . . .

As translators, Tom and ourselves were to be reassured.

You must make it clear to yourself that none of the future variations for the publication of *Gulag* will in any way infringe on your merits as a translator, or your interests. Everything else it seems to me is a purely formal judicial consideration. As for Harper & Row they will have received enough profit even from the American edition alone. . . .

And there was surely need for reassurance, since in the same letter Eva quoted the message from Solzhenitsyn, written the previous October, the message she had been in no hurry to pass on to us.

"I am especially sensitive to English translations (once I completed courses for translators from English)—and to speak honestly *I am not pleased* with any of the big translations. Some of them bring me to despair. Meanwhile, a lot else will soon depend on how the translations of *August, October, March* and . . . [*Gulag*] will be understood and received. This is not simply my author's sensibility, from this the whole solidity of my legs depends, and I cannot give in to *anyone* out of good feelings. You may simply quote this passage to [O.A.C.]. . . ."

In other words, the translation arranged for and edited by us—as well as all other English translations—had displeased the author; yet paradoxically, we were to work in the very role in which Solzhenitsyn appeared to believe we had given him feet of clay.

Eva's letter convinced me that immediate disengagement was the only course left open to us.

Early in February 1973 I returned to a wintery Connecticut and on the tenth of that month, after talks with Henry and with Tony, I wrote in English to Solzhenitsyn:

Dear Alexander Issayevich,

As we informed you in September we cannot continue work on the manuscript under an arrangement of divided responsibility for its translation and publication. Therefore, since we have now learned that you wish to proceed only in this manner, we must irrevocably relinquish all existing rights and responsibilities with respect to the translation and publication of this work.

We do this in the belief that, under the circumstances which now prevail, our resignation at this time is in your best interests, for we foresee only difficulties and dangers in maintaining a partnership role. Our reasons are principally these:

1. In sharing the job with your acknowledged representative and others the risk of disclosure of all our past and present activities on your behalf would be unacceptably high; both with respect to you and other friends involved.

2. In resigning the power to contract for world rights on your behalf we lose the power to achieve the quality of worldwide publication, such as was obtained in the case of the other work.

3. The shared responsibility system would inevitably be attended by an endless succession of unproductive complexities, harmful to the success of publication, and, again, likely to lead to disclosures.

Believe us, this decision is the most difficult one we have had to make in five and a half years of hard choices arising from our custodianship of the two works. We hope that you will understand our reasons for taking this step, just as we believe we understand why you have taken those which make it necessary. There was a time for our work in helping to make your name and one of your books known around the world; we have done the best job we could, working within the restrictions of secrecy, but now we feel that it is time to step aside, leaving a clear path for your acknowledged representative to proceed with the publication of the great works yet to come.

The English translation of the current manuscript is now finished in the state of a first draft and a substantial part in more finished style. The translation is the property of Mr. Thomas Whitney, and Dr. Heeb should enter into negotiations with him concerning its completion and disposition. We are certain that you will understand why it is now impossible for us to continue in the role of cotranslators.

It is with a sense of sadness that we disengage from services on behalf of the publication of your works, but it is also with a certain pride in having played some part in making your work widely known. At a time of insidious repression of human rights and dignity, when people of good will know only impotence and alienation, your voice has sounded clearly and strongly, bringing the hope that man is not yet condemned to abandon his destiny to deaf powers. The force of this message has been felt throughout the world. Many people who could only clumsily pronounce your name knew at once that yours was no ordinary voice, that your work reaches out urgently from print and paper to consciousness. First there were tens of thousands, now there are tens of millions. Yes, we are indeed proud to have aided in bringing your words to a great audience.

Of your work to date we believe that the one to which we especially refer now has a value that reaches beyond literature and beyond the ordinary limitations of history. It is, without any doubt, a very great and unique monument to the human spirit. That we shall not contribute to the final phases of its publication is a matter of deep regret to us; but for the reasons set forth above we believe that our complete disengagement at this time is necessary. Again, we make this difficult choice, as we have made all others, in the belief that it is the best and safest course with respect to you and certain other friends. We hope that we are right, we cannot be certain; but right or wrong we hope fervently that you will sense our undiminished devotion to you and to your work.

We dispatched this letter via Dr. Heeb. It was to be two months before it would make its way to Solzhenitsyn.

In early April I accepted a journalistic assignment which brought me into a Soviet environment very different from any I had ever known. A women's magazine had asked me to travel on the first regular Atlantic crossing of the passenger liner *Mikhail Lermontov*, joining the ship for its westward run and writing my impressions of the voyage. As I flew out of Kennedy bound for Le Havre to meet the ship, the Watergate scandal was beginning to unfold. Its uproar did not reach the *Lermontov*. In fact, no echo of unpleasantness anywhere disturbed the festive new liner with its round-the-clock schedule of activities, an endless succession of folk dances, teas, games, copious meals. Outside, the seas were heavy, the waves tossed icebergs, but the *Lermontov*, scientifically stablized, plowed ahead, under the command of her captain, a superb seaman adored by his crew, the perfect master of a perfect vessel. It was like an ideal kindergarten, where by some miracle the children—crew and passengers alike—were well behaved at all times.

On this voyage I found it strange to think of Alexander Solzhenitsyn and Andrei Sakharov in the real Soviet world. My admiration for their ability to make their voices heard was stronger than ever; but I also understood the thousands of other Russians—writers, scientists, intellectuals in positions of power— who had been lulled to silence by a comfortable existence, an existence threatened on all sides by the freezing waves and icebergs of the Gulag Archipelago.

Despite my numerous absences, my reunions with Henry were always joyful. This particular return was especially happy. I felt that we were on the eve of a new life, one in which we could perhaps continue to work to help the mission of Solzhenitsyn, Sakharov, and other dissidents—but in some new way, on our own terms.

Soon after my return, I received a reply to my February letter of resignation. It was in Russian with some phrases in English (they are in quotation marks in the literal translation that follows) and both the sender and the addressee were unnamed.

April 5, 1973
(Alas, your letter took two months
to reach me.)

Dear ———:

Your letter has greatly saddened me, especially for its lack of correspondence with the *spirit* of the book we are now talking about. I cannot suppose that during the five years of your contact with it you could have remained indifferent to this spirit and not have been in some measure seized by it. However your letter which has just arrived seems to hold that very spirit in contempt.

All these months your arguments have been sporadically passed along to me to the effect that you perceived some kind of disagreement; I could not understand them exactly. I could not understand: why should the fate of this book be decided not by the fate of its much-suffering population, not by the problems and plans of its author, but by the interest of some kind of commercial publishing house, which according to our agreements SHOULD HAVE KNOWN NOTHING OF IT UNTIL THIS DAY (but—it does?). Now your letter has arrived, and in three points the disagreement is formulated. However, I am rereading these points and, you will pardon me, I see no disagreement. They do NOT exist. Or possibly they are not named by you. Point three simply reiterates point one, "risk of disclosures." But it is in fact the OTHER WAY AROUND: limiting yourself to ONLY the role of a translator, of ONLY one edition, you ensure with a hundred percent certainty NONdisclosure for yourself and those close to you. The risk of disclosure would be great were you to take full authority of a worldwide representation (especially in the event of conflict or trial). Because the publication will not be regulated by a publishing house chosen by you but by my attorney, why should you become known? Precisely behind his back you will be invisible. A "shared responsibility system" was not considered: you are FULLY responsible but ONLY for your own translation. Point two is also inconsistent: has the struggle around the last book not demonstrated that today NO ONE except my lawyer with full powers can defend my rights? And on the contrary, when your publishing house in the case of the first book had the power for world rights this in no way allowed it to "achieve the quality of worldwide publication"; it is enough to remember the French edition and I do not enter into the appraisal of other translations and of the film.

The fate of THIS book must be completely special: the translators will not be chosen by the publishing house but by us (almost all of them by me PERSONALLY). The translators having accomplished their work will, only toward the very end of it, recommend appropriate publishing houses. Moreover the majority of publishing houses will cringe from my unusual conditions (you will be told about them). Under these conditions, the publishing house will have EXTREMELY SMALL profits. This must be, so that this book will not become a commercial commodity, will not be sold at demented Western prices. ($10! This is 60 rubles. This cannot even be conceived by our compatriots!) I'll tell you frankly, judging by the first book and all the activity of the publishing house which you defend, I infer with great certainty that it will NOT like my conditions.

Thus, participating in the present work constitutes for you in the future an object of rather considerable pride for you, stronger than the arguments enumerated in your letter. And I ask you VERY much to think over and over your decision for which I have not received any valid reason and perhaps renounce this decision. I will be sincerely happy if you keep for yourself the right of translation, to be ready at the agreed upon date—without going beyond the limitations of my conditions for all translators and all publishing houses.

If to our general regret your decision should be irreversible, I see one way of terminating the affair, just for all and offensive to no one: FIRE.* Your greatly unfinished work (because a literal translation I cannot even consider the beginning of a translation, it being a stage which is usually completely unnecessary for translators) cannot be considered the "property of T.W." as you write since and insofar as this work is paid for (the estimation of it you will conduct with Dr. H.). His "property" could only be the right to put his NAME on the FINISHED work, and only that. Doing the raw work is not coauthorship, nor can coauthors be matched by the will of circumstance, but only by harmony of opinions. Thus, upon completion of payment, if this has not yet been done, all the materials of the translation must be, by you personally or by your representative, BURNED, let us say inside the fireplace of Dr. H. and in his presence. (Under these circumstances, what to do with the Russian original—whether to throw it in the fire or to give it to Dr. H.—I confer this choice upon you, but in no third form should any copy be left to exist.) I am in agreement with

---

* Who can GIVE AWAY his work to someone else to finish? Who will accept strange raw materials to finish? The only thing that remains is to consider the work UNDONE, therefore—fire.

either outcome although it would be a shame to confer absurdity on the heroic feat of Mr. X. [in carrying out the Russian original]. The translation into your tongue will be started from ZERO—and in no other way. The only consequence will be a certain delay of that language by comparison with the others. Never mind. I see no reason for "conversations" between Dr. H. and T.W., I see no "completion" of a work which has been left in a chaotic state, we shall not discuss this.

I feel bitter that for some completely secondary, unnamed reasons you have determined to put a spot on the movement of this book, which is not a literary commodity but a link in Russian history. And today your own decision also will become a link in it.

My most heartfelt good wishes—to all whom I know personally!

I received this letter on a clear, bright day in May 1973. As I read its tightly packed typewritten lines, with both my name and Solzhenitsyn's omitted, I could not believe my eyes. I still couldn't believe them as I read the letter to Henry. I could not quite believe that this letter actually came from Solzhenitsyn.

"Does Dr. Heeb's office *have* a fireplace?" Henry asked when I had finished.

I was not amused. Here, in place of the author of *One Day*, the man who had asked for my aid and exulted when it bore fruit, was an authoritarian figure who thought nothing of attacking those who had helped him, none more virulently than those in the West. Their contribution must be ceremoniously burned. All trace incinerated, just as, in *Gulag One*, the tons of seized documents are burned in the Lubyanka furnaces to rain as fine ash on the prisoners.

The power which had been given to me in 1967, which had then been exercised in the West, must be returned to Solzhenitsyn—as if it had never left his hands. The tainted power must destroy itself. It must be purified by fire.

As for the other members of the American secret circle, they were apparently to be dismissed without a word of greeting, much less thanks.

179

That very evening I wrote a indignant answer to Solzhenitsyn. The words came quickly.

May 9, 1973

Dear Alexander Issayevich,

In other, earlier times I would have asked my father to avenge my honor on receiving your letter of April 5, 1973, knowing of course that he would do everything possible to avoid killing a great Russian writer in a duel! You insinuate that I have fallen prey to commercialism in acting, on your request, as trustee for your books: "Why should the fate of this book be decided not by the fate of its much-suffering population, not by the problems and plans of its author, but by the interest of some kind of commercial publishing house, which according to our agreements should have known nothing of it until this day (but—it does?)."

First, I want to remind you that I mentioned the existence of your book only because you gave me express permission to do so through third parties of impeccable reliability, before witnesses—and only for the purpose of serving your publishing interests. This was to cause us endless, unnecessary difficulties.

Let me also declare solemnly that the "commercial" means used in publishing *The First Circle* were not for the benefit of any publishing firm or my own, but only in order to make you known in the West, and to help you receive the Nobel prize. What I regret and fear—for your sake—is your lack of true information.

An important engagement that we made at your request, within the secret circle working for you, was translation. We *cannot go back* on agreements made earlier, with your authorization, and verified with you. I cannot act with persons I have made contracts with in the manner you suggest in your letter. You do not seem to understand that our circle was (and still is) cemented, not by a love of dollars, but by a love of Russia.*

---

* For more than six years' work between 1967 and 1973, Henry and I together received from Solzhenitsyn's trust compensation in the form of commissions and fees for editorial work amounting to an annual average of $11,800. My involvement in the trust's affairs was to continue for two years, during which I received no payment.

Our own reasons for desisting from the editing of your book is that we realize that our work has not satisfied you. [Eva] made this clear in a letter dated Jan. 27, 1973 in which she quoted your own words on the subject. We can only work according to our own standards, in our own way. The results in the case of the first book received high acclaim in the United States.

The present book is magnificent and unique. I am sensitive to its spirit. It contains the best you have to offer. It is an homage to your characters, your anonymous helpers. I hope that you can publish it in exactly the manner you want, and at the date you choose.

In the light of the spirit of your book, the honor of our circle, which served Russia through you for five years, is clear.

We did not burn the translation of *Gulag*. Instead, we set about putting Dr. Heeb in direct contact with Tom Whitney and concluding all remaining business of the Solzhenitsyn trust. That spring, Dr. Heeb announced his intention of visiting the United States and, after several postponements, owing to his political past, arrived with his wife in New York in June 1973.

22

Tony showed the visitors from Zurich the sights of Manhattan and, on a radiant sunny day, brought them to our house in Connecticut.

By then, the details of our disengagement had been worked out between the two lawyers, and luncheon in the country was mainly ceremonial. The principal business was to be the presentation of our copy of the Russian manuscript of *The Gulag Archipelago* to its new steward.

On the way to our house, Tony and the Heebs stopped off at Tom's to meet and to discuss the translation.

As I was getting ready for our guests' arrival that morning, I remember preparing a green salad and looking out on the dappled sunshine in the birch woods outside the kitchen window.

I recalled the dream of the soldier-trees invading the house. Now the trees were in place. I arranged green pears on a blue platter. I was composing paintings in my head. For six years I had lived in an outpost of Solzhenitsyn's world. Now, with Dr. Heeb arriving to pick up the Russian text, I could soon paint the pears, the birches, return to neglected pursuits. When Tony's car turned into our drive, I felt a wave of relief that my responsibilities would soon, at last, be passed to other hands.

At this lunch, Dr. Heeb seemed a little more at ease than he had been in Switzerland. His wife was less reserved than he, and more interested in things American. Conversation was cordial. Tony was his usual genial self. We were pleased to be ending our secret relationship with Solzhenitsyn; Dr. Heeb was pleased to be assuming undisputed control of the world rights to his masterpiece.

I had written Solzhenitsyn in February about the status of the English translation. Now, over coffee, we explained the situation to Dr. Heeb in greater detail. Tom had completed a translation of the entire three volumes. We had edited the first, acting in place of the publisher's editors, as we had done in the case of *The First Circle*. We assured him that the translation was sufficiently advanced so that, on Solzhenitsyn's signal, volume one of *Gulag* could be rushed into print. Harper & Row was prepared to assist Tom in readying the manuscript without delay.

We explained these matters—which were to be of crucial importance in our relationship with Solzhenitsyn—to Dr. Heeb, who signified he understood them.

After lunch, we took our visitors on a short stroll along the paths around our house. Soon it was time for Tony to drive the Heebs back to the city. Henry brought the manuscript in a leather-handled Mexican travel bag and gave it to Dr. Heeb. As he was getting into the car, the lawyer thanked him, adding mildly,

"*Après tout, cher Monsieur, nous sommes tous des serviteurs.*"

As Tony and the guests drove off, I walked back to the house with Henry, the birch leaves now luminescent in the golden afternoon light. I felt then that my world was there to paint again—yet Dr. Heeb's parting words hung in the air, incongruous and a little threatening:

"After all, dear sir, we are all servants."

23

THROUGHOUT 1971 and 1972, Solzhenitsyn had been living—in his own words—a camouflaged existence, buying time to advance his work on the novel about World War I and the Revolution. Harassed by police officials over the question of residence permits, he had been staying at the house of the cellist Mstislav Rostropovich, who, after Chukovsky's death, offered shelter and, as long as he could, the shield of his international fame.

The Gulag Archipelago, according to its author's plan at the time, was not to appear until May 1975.

In June 1973, while Dr. Heeb was in the United States, the struggle between Solzhenitsyn and "our people," as he ironically referred to Soviet officialdom, took a new turn. He entered a phase in which he saw himself and Andrei Sakharov, independently of one another, involved with the government in a battle of "meeting engagements," a military term meaning blind combat in which each side maneuvers without advance knowledge of the other's positions. Anonymous letters with threats against him and his family and demands for large sums of money appeared in Solzhenitsyn's mail, letters he knew were penned by "pseudogangsters" in government pay. Against such intimidation, he held his ground, skirmishing with the authorities while pressing on with his writing. In August, he calculated that he needed only four months, until the end of the year, to finish the second "knot" of the novel, some of whose chapters dealt with the founder of the Soviet state, V. I. Lenin.

New arrests of dissidents stirred Moscow. The ignominious show-trial of Yakir and Krassin was staged. Solzhenitsyn, casting around for a way to "shake up the West" (as he put it in his memoir, *How the Calf Butted the Oak*), hit upon the plan of addressing a letter to the Soviet leaders, calling upon them to reject the lies and the crippling "foreign"—that is, Marxist— ideology of the recent past. Why not strike out on a course charted by realism rooted in morality and religion? Interrupting work on the novel, he plunged into drafting these ideas in a "Letter to the Soviet Leaders."

On August 21, Andrei Sakharov, at a press conference, declared, "the USSR is a vast concentration camp, a vast detention zone."

At the same time, in Leningrad, a tragedy was unfolding. Elizaveta Denisovna Voronianskaya had once been a devoted, almost worshipful assistant to Solzhenitsyn. Into her hands he had passed a copy of *The Gulag Archipelago* for safekeeping. Later, when he was assured that the microfilm had reached us (and possibly that a third had reached Dr. Heeb), he had ordered Voronianskaya to destroy the copy in her possession. Probably fearing that other copies would be apprehended, she had not done so. That summer she was arrested, interrogated, and eventually forced to reveal the location of the hidden copy. Soon after her release, she hanged herself in her apartment.

Now, *The Gulag Archipelago*, the work that comprehensively and eloquently documented Sakharov's charge that the USSR was a concentration camp, the work that its author had been convinced he would pay for with his life, was in the possession of the KGB.

At no moment is the intensity of Solzhenitsyn's sense of mission more evident than in his response to this apparent catastrophe.

He was elated.

The successive postponements of the publication of *Gulag* had weighed heavily on him. Now a dire event had signaled that the time of total confrontation had arrived. The death of a disobedient assistant was like the snuffing out of one candle flame among millions. It told him that *now* he was committed to avenge all the victims of Soviet terror. This was the ultimate campaign. He took up the challenge joyously.

In *How the Calf Butted the Oak*, Solzhenitsyn was to write of this moment:

Now there will be many blows, given and taken, but I too stand so much stronger, and for the first time, *the first time,* I go into battle at my full stature, in my full voice.

. . . For *my* life—it is a great moment, this engagement, for which, perhaps, I have been living. (And were the sound of these battles to die away? To go away for years into the depths of the countryside, among fields, sky, forest, horses—to write my novel at leisure. . . .)

But—for *them*? Has not the time come at last, when Russia will begin to wake up? Is this not the moment out of those prescient subterranean visions when *Birnam wood will move*?

It is likely that there are once again mistakes in my forecasting and in my calculations. There are many things at close range that I still do not see. The Higher Hand will correct me in many ways. But this does not cloud my breast. What gladdens me and strengthens me is that I do not invent and implement everything, that I am—only a sword, well-sharpened, against an impure power, magically empowered to cut it up and disperse it.

Oh God grant me not to break under the blows! Not to fall from your hand!

On September 5, Alexander Solzhenitsyn dispatched the "Letter to the Soviet Leaders." On his wife's advice, he delayed sending copies to the West; the leaders must first be given a chance to respond. He would wait a little before confronting the West with his manifesto.

But on that same day, he issued the long-deferred order concerning *The Gulag Archipelago*:

"Publish immediately."

ON SEPTEMBER 4, one day before the signal to publish was given to him by Solzhenitsyn, Dr. Heeb wrote, in part, to Tony:

> I beg you and Mrs. Carlisle to send to me the first part of our friend's K2 in English translation. You remember that we agreed that the translation made by Mr. T.W. should be used. But after Mrs. Carlisle's decision to resign it seems necessary that any other expert can be found. For that purpose I should possess a part of the translation. I would be very grateful to you if you would send me the first part as soon as possible.

When this letter reached Tony, Henry and I were on Nantucket, where we had gone for a long holiday marking our first summer away from the Italian Opera. But even as we were settling in, extraordinary events had begun unfolding in Moscow. By means of radio broadcasts, newspaper stories, and communications from friends in Europe, we were now avidly following every battle in the Soviet authorities' war against Sakharov and Solzhenitsyn. By the time a copy of Dr. Heeb's letter was forwarded to us, Henry and I already knew the details of Elizaveta Voronianskaye's suicide and understood that at last the publication of *Gulag* was at hand.

I wrote to Tony in New York, telling him that we should be sending to Dr. Heeb not only the first part of Tom's translation, as requested by Heeb, but the entire English text of *Gulag* as well, so that, without loss of time, the Zurich expert might judge the work as a whole. I also asked Tony to let Heeb know that the first volume of *Gulag*, which Henry and I had edited, was at his disposal. I was ready to ship it to him immediately.

But Tony, who was in frequent touch with Dr. Heeb at that time, felt otherwise. He reported to me that Dr. Heeb, for reasons of his own, was pointedly not requesting the part of *Gulag* translated by Tom and edited by Henry and myself. However, to assuage my doubts, Tony wrote to Dr. Heeb again, querying him on what he wanted.

Dr. Heeb's reply was prompt. Telephoning Tony, Heeb told him that the Whitney translation was what he wanted, and all three volumes, since they were available. As for the first volume of the work edited by us, it was not at that time needed.

I was baffled and queried Tony again. He was positive about Heeb's response. Phoning me on Nantucket, Tony reviewed his telephone conversations with Dr. Heeb and, as a reminder, quoted from the September 4 letter: "You remember that we agreed that the translation made by Mr. T.W. should be used."

The two men had by then agreed that Tony would deliver the entire Whitney translation personally to Dr. Heeb in Zurich on October 17.

On October 30, having solicited an expert opinion of the translation, Dr. Heeb wrote to Tony. His letter read in part:

I am very glad to inform you that the acceptability of the translation by Mr. Whitney is established. There appears to be a small number of omissions. These are the normal oversight such as are common to all translators and consist only of phrases, but it would be as well to put them in. There are also a sprinkling of mistakes. These are not usually very serious and consist mainly of inexactitudes or of misunderstandings of Soviet prison terminology, but it would be best to correct them. Our expert says finally, that light editing in English can also cope with the problems of style.

So I beg you to inform Mr. Whitney and to tell me as soon as possible if he agrees that his manuscript can be corrected in this sense and then be published.

At last I beg you to let me know which remuneration must be paid to Mr. Whitney.*

During the fall and into the winter, we and the other members of the secret circle stood aside while Dr. Heeb, acting for his client, conducted lengthy negotiations with Harper & Row. "I infer with great certainty," Solzhenitsyn had written me in April, "that [Harper & Row] will NOT like my conditions." We looked on in despair as all our preparations for the swift publication of the first volume in the United States fell to pieces.

Only in December did Dr. Heeb enter into a contract with Harper & Row, and only then could final revision proceed and publication be scheduled.

Harper & Row assigned Frances Lindley to edit the book. Meanwhile, Solzhenitsyn had assigned an additional collaborator, Michael Scammel, to work with Tom. But Scammel had other duties to perform for Solzhenitsyn before he was free to apply himself to the task, and so further delay ensued.

Our impression at the time was that orders were being issued from Moscow via Zurich, the effect of which was, intentionally or otherwise, to slow publication of *The Gulag Archipelago* in the English language. Despite the favorable opinion of Dr. Heeb's expert, Solzhenitsyn seemed determined to justify his assertion, based on no evidence of any kind, that Tom's translation was in "a chaotic state." In his letter in which he ordered me to burn that translation, he had written: "The only consequence will be a certain delay of that language by comparison with the others. Never mind." Was that now his intention?

---

* Tom's immense labor in bringing forth the highly acclaimed translation of volumes one and two of *The Gulag Archipelago* was a contribution to Solzhenitsyn's mission. He asked for and received no remuneration for it.

24

Soon after the order to publish *Gulag* had been issued, the Solzhenitsyns found themselves living in Moscow in a state of siege. Harassments intensified, followed by ominous periods of calm. On February 12, 1974, the embattled author was arrested, stripped of his nationality, and summarily thrown out of the motherland. On his arrival in Frankfurt he carried a single pink rose given him by a well-wisher. This flower seemed to symbolize the huge wave of public support which greeted him in the West. He was welcomed like a Lindbergh, a world hero just landed after a long, perilous journey.

In March, shortly after his expulsion, I was again in Europe on a writing assignment. I decided to ask whether I could call on him in Zurich. To my note requesting a meeting came a postcard by return mail:

191

I can receive [you] for a couple of hours on Thursday, March 21, around 2 or 3 o'clock in the afternoon. If this is inconvenient, do call my lawyer—but it would be best not to make changes. Indeed there is a lot to talk about—speaking honestly, if the American edition had come out in January—they would not have dared to throw me out of Russia.

I was stunned. In Geneva, at breakfast over coffee, I read and reread Solzhenitsyn's words, written in his neat, spidery handwriting. The coffee was growing cold in my cup. In my worst dreams about what might befall our enterprise I had never imagined anything quite like this. Could he really be maintaining that we had been responsible for the delay in the American publication of *The Gulag Archipelago*?

I remember, on a cold gray afternoon, wandering through a show of Russian icons in a Geneva museum, hardly seeing them, wondering about these questions—and about my relationship with this awesome man I was soon to meet again. The golden Virgins and saints seemed to look at me with sympathy, figures expressive of that compassion which runs deep in Russian religious tradition. Under the gaze of their lifelike eyes, little by little my anger subsided, leaving only a taste of the pervasive sadness I had first felt during that summer afternoon over the Atlantic when I became aware of Solzhenitsyn's repudiation.

The next day I traveled by train to Zurich. It was a clear morning, the official first day of spring and also the first real spring day. Out the window, the landscape was a painting by Paul Klee, the mountain slopes, still under a thin layer of snow with patches of green showing through, were dotted with graphic signs—fences, cattle, stone barns with pointed tiled roofs. During the long ride I tried to work on a manuscript I was finishing, but neither my writing nor the scenery could take my mind off the thought that had haunted me since I had received the postcard: For a Russian writer, exile is a devastating blow. And Solzhenitsyn was blaming me for the catastrophe that had befallen him.

Suddenly I thought of Potapov, the nearsighted engineer in

The First Circle. In his youth, Potapov had helped build the Dnieproges dam, a triumph of early Soviet technology. He had fought the Germans heroically in World War II. After the war, he was accused by Soviet authorities of having sold the Dnieproges dam to the German High Command and sent to a camp for this crime. Somehow the thought restored me. Potapov had borne the absurd accusation with resignation and even humor.

I arrived in Zurich about two o'clock in the afternoon and took a taxi. The ride was exhilarating; I had the feeling of being lifted high above the city in a matter of moments, being carried from the grimly elegant downtown into an airy world of gardens and cozy homes. We stopped at Stapferstrasse 45.

The sun was very warm. I stood before a typical European suburban villa, with a narrow metal gate, a hedge, a garden, the stucco house beyond, sheltered by large shade trees.

The gate was locked. I couldn't find a doorbell. The house was too far to call out. I stood there, four or five minutes, a painful sense of déjà vu rising in me, perhaps of some submerged memory of Moscow, where so many entryways are forbidding. There was something very disheartening about this small iron gate. Or was it some recollection out of my childhood in the suburbs of Paris? Suddenly I wanted to run—down the hill to the railroad station, as I had run across the plaza to the hotel after my first meeting with Solzhenitsyn. I wanted to run now.

Instead, I went on searching for a doorbell. I tried banging on the gate with my fist.

The next thing I remember was Solzhenitsyn, opening the gate, shaking my hand, inviting me to step into the garden. At once I felt a surge of gladness. He was in Zurich, as vigorous as he had been in Moscow. Perhaps our misunderstandings could be cleared up as easily as the gate had been opened.

As Solzhenitsyn looked at me I saw that he no longer masked his habit of closely studying the person he was with. The youthful, dynamic man I had met in Moscow was now an imperious figure, part military, part ecclesiastical, with a priestly beard and eyes more scrutinizing than ever. For an instant I had the feeling of being a junior lieutenant reporting to a commander in chief, an acolyte entering the presence of a prince of the church. His greeting was markedly cordial, but I knew at once that I was no longer a friend.

In view of his postcard I had expected no warm welcome from Solzhenitsyn, and I was relieved that he was as genial as he was. He showed me along a narrow path to the house. What struck me most about him was his carefully bridled exhilaration. I could sense it in his springy walk, the carriage of his head. I had felt this joyous inner force in Moscow, but now he seemed intent upon holding it in check. It colored his every movement and seemed to arise from a closely guarded sense of triumph.

Near the house, in the sunshine under a tall tree still free of leaves, stood a kitchen chair. To my surprise, he sat down on it and took out a tiny notebook.

"It will take but a second. I have something to finish," he said and wrote rapidly in his tiny handwriting as I stood by. The commander in chief was a guerrilla leader jotting a note on the day's operations. Then, a moment later, he was up again, showing me in.

Inside, as out, the house was like any villa in an affluent European suburb. It was dark and cool. Solzhenitsyn had only recently moved into it. In the front parlor there was little furniture—a table, chairs, a child's crib, a high chair, half uncrated. Books and manuscripts were stacked on the floor in big piles. Solzhenitsyn had me settle on a chair with my back to a window and sat facing me.

"How is your family, Alexander Issayevich?" I asked.

"Very well," he said. "I speak with my wife every day on the telephone. Little Styopa has been ill but he's better now."

"And when are they expected to reach Zurich?"

"My wife is packing my archives."

In the bright light from the window, despite his iron control, triumph showed in his face. "She will not leave the USSR unless the archives are allowed out too. That is final. Because of this, Olga Vadimovna, the date of her arrival is not known."

I remember telling him almost at once that the delay in the

publication of the American edition of the first volume of *The Gulag Archipelago* was in no way our doing, or Tom Whitney's, or Harper & Row's. I described how Dr. Heeb had proceeded, adding that if the right to contract and arrange for final editing had been left in our hands, volume one would have already appeared in English.

Solzhenitsyn was listening intently, his face cold and set. Sitting straight on my hard-backed chair, I told him in detail of the English translation of *Gulag*. I told him of the existence of the two versions of volume one, of how the edited version had not been requested, of the slow pace at which Michael Scammel had been proceeding with his work on Tom's translation. As I spoke, Potapov's example receded. The anger that had seized me on receiving Solzhenitsyn's postcard was again rising. With great effort, I controlled it, recalling my last encounter with him on that Moscow balcony. I had seen then that he was the sort of man who respects firmness above all. So, as I spoke about the events, about dates and publishing arrangements that, despite their complexity, were intimately familiar to me, I forced myself to remain calm.

And then I noticed that the inscrutable face, the somber demeanor, seemed to soften. I felt that Solzhenitsyn, who must really have let himself believe that I had delayed American publication of *Gulag* and thus caused his expulsion, was now prepared to accept my explanations. Little by little, the imperious chieftain was giving way to the younger, more responsive Solzhenitsyn of former years.

After a while he got up and invited me into a small kitchen for tea. He struggled with an electric stove he was not yet familiar with, but eventually the kettle boiled and we sat across from each other at the small kitchen table, over steaming cups.

He started to tell me about the attacks which he and Dr. Sakharov had successfully repelled in August and September of the previous year. Then suddenly he broke off and was on his feet, remembering something. Another note to jot, I wondered? Instead, he returned with a large square tin box containing cookies of every imaginable kind and offered them. I took one. The variety of choice clearly delighted him. He chose one too.

"At first we fought our separate battles," he went on. "There had been no advance synchronization. Bullets were flying." He urged me to take another cookie, then his face suddenly darkened. "You wrote to me about a duel when I was under real fire, and you were taking no risk whatever."

I answered, "Alexander Issayevich, in your letter you accused us of betraying the spirit of your book. You accused us of telling the publisher about it when no one should have known of it—yet *you yourself asked me to tell them.* In January of 1968. We were dedicated to the spirit of your books—and dismayed when you accused us of commercialism. I was deeply wounded. That was why I wrote you as I did."

"I told you to tell the publisher?"

"In 1968."

"I may have," he said at last, grudgingly, presenting me with the cookie tin. "Yes, I seem to remember that I did, now that you mention it."

He got up and, restlessly pacing the kitchen floor, resumed his account of the events of the previous summer and fall. He spoke of skirmishes and counterattacks and victories. Of gunsmoke and salvos. As he talked I was aware that he said nothing about the most heartbreaking event of that time, the death in Leningrad of the woman who had taken her life after being forced to reveal the cache of *The Gulag Archipelago* manuscript.

He told me how the KGB had burned his camp jacket.

"My wife went immediately to the prison to try to retrieve it, but it was too late. They are fetishists, those policemen. They must have felt that in destroying my old *bushlak* they were destroying me." Lightly he touched his brand-new, Swiss-made, blue ski jacket, which lay over a chair. "I do miss it," he added.

And suddenly, in an insistent voice: "Olga Vadimovna, had *The Gulag Archipelago* come out in time they never would have dared expel me! I had a fabulous strategy worked out, all ready to be set in motion. A whole campaign . . ." There was a fierce longing for battle in his words. He had not believed me, after all.

"Alexander Issayevich, nothing should have prevented Dr. Heeb from directing Harper & Row to publish volume one in January of this year. Perhaps there was some breakdown in communication between you and him."

He listened, nodding. Once again, I had the feeling that he believed me—for the moment.

The afternoon was advancing, the kitchen was growing dark. I remarked to myself then that Solzhenitsyn made no further inquiry about my six eventful years as his representative.

At the same time, the tension between us eased. With that intensity which I took to be repressed inner joy, he spoke rapidly of his current concerns—he was about to come out with a barrage of new publications—touching briefly on a topic, then dropping it abruptly and taking up another.

Alexander Ford's film of *The First Circle* had displeased him. "Why had Ford been chosen?"

"Because your own appointed intermediary said that you approved of him," I told him in surprise.

"Perhaps. Perhaps I did say that. An author should have had absolute artistic control in such a situation, though. I hope for this in the future."

When I started to explain that, short of producing the film himself, an author never has complete artistic control over a motion picture, Solzhenitsyn, to my astonishment, repeated, for a third time, the accusation that we had stalled the American publication of *The Gulag Archipelago*.

This time, exasperated, I said sharply, "Look at the dates, Alexander Issayevich. We were not at that time empowered to have anything to do with publishing *Gulag*. Dr. Heeb was in charge. He had full control—under your orders."

As he had done in the street in Moscow in 1967, he searched my face closely. And for a third time seemed satisfied.

He asked me to send him a detailed account of the film negotiations for *The First Circle*. Then he spoke about the ninety-six-chapter version of that novel. He had released certain of the unpublished chapters shortly before his expulsion. He had done this as a test of strength against the authorities, at a time when the USSR was signing the Universal Copyright Convention. He understood that he should not undermine Harper & Row's control of world copyright. He was sorry he had had to do this. He said, "The reason I sent them out was not to counter Harper & Row but to challenge the repressive Soviet interpretation of the new copyright laws."

Then, suddenly his face clouded again. This time he spoke with great violence against the *New York Times*.

During his years of siege in the USSR, while he was under the guns of the KGB, no voice in the West had been better informed or more eloquent than the *Times* in defending Solzhenitsyn and making his mission known around the world. Through special news reports and editorials, the paper consistently championed him. Now, it had published a summary, with excerpts, of an unedited version of his "Letter to the Soviet Leaders"—a version containing attacks against the West and apparently intended for the attention of the leaders only—after having declined to buy a modified version of the text offered to them for Western publication by Michael Scammel, who, through the Curtis Brown agency, had named a considerable price. To Solzhenitsyn, the years of passionate advocacy by the *Times* for his cause were wiped out in a single sweep.

"They accuse me of nationalism when, on the contrary, I want Russia to return all her acquired dominions, such as the Ukraine and Estonia, to their people. They don't know what they're talking about!"

The two hours I had spent in the villa seemed to have vanished in an instant. It was time for me to go. Yet when I started to get up my host gestured for me to stay.

Without blaming me this time, he returned to the matter of his exile. "It was such a blow. I was ready with such a thundering bombardment!" He told me that he planned the next period of his life to be one of intensive writing and publishing. He would astound the world with a succession of new books. In all that he said I was aware more than ever of that joy held in an iron grip.

Soon there was no more time if I was to return to Geneva that evening. Solzhenitsyn helped me on with my coat and put on his ski jacket. A gray, moist twilight was descending on Zurich as he walked me to a nearby trolley. "It's faster than a cab," he said. In his precise manner he explained where to get out near the railroad station. I was to look for a cluster of pine trees against an embankment. I couldn't miss it. We walked downhill toward the trolley stop. Once again, as I had done in Moscow, I observed Solzhenitsyn's zek ability to make himself inconspicuous as he moved along a city street. In his ski jacket, walking with a smooth, rapid step, Alexander Solzhenitsyn was suddenly no more. In his place was only an ordinary Zurich passerby on his way downtown.

At the stop he got me a ticket from one of those electronic machines that only natives of Switzerland know how to operate. We said goodbye hastily as the multi-wagoned trolley crawled up to the curb like a huge caterpillar. I got in and looked back over my shoulder as it pulled away. I was about to wave goodbye to Solzhenitsyn but he had disappeared into the gray Zurich dusk.

ABOUT A WEEK LATER, as I was getting ready to leave Paris for home, I received an unsealed message from Solzhenitsyn via the YMCA Press:

Olga Vadimovna, I am very sorry that during the week you were able to come to Zurich, Dr. Heeb was absent and I had no information to counter yours during our conversation. Upon his return I have learned: that in June 1973 he requested that you give him the English translation, but you answered that you could not do this without Tom Whitney's consent and in view of the lack of final readiness of the translation; that in October 1973, having received three volumes of "translation," Dr. Heeb was not informed—and has learned from me only now—that this was a so-called "unedited translation," and that the work of your collective on Volume I was never shown to him.

I sat down on the terrace of a café with this letter opened before me on the small round table. The café, in a working-class section of town, reminded me of the Paris of my childhood. It was filled with men in blue overalls from nearby workshops, with pretty young secretaries enjoying their lunch break. Once, Russian painters living in that part of the city had gathered in this café, but now I was the only Russian there.

Barely aware of the midday din, I was studying Solzhenitsyn's angry note. If Solzhenitsyn was quoting Dr. Heeb accurately, then the best I could believe was that Heeb himself had misunderstood all my efforts to clarify the situation on *Gulag*. Yet knowing Solzhenitsyn's own inconsistencies and seeming misperceptions, I could not be sure it was Heeb who was at fault. Hoping to make sense of it all, I took a notebook out of my purse and, on a blank page, listed the charges:

1. According to Solzhenitsyn, Dr. Heeb was saying that in June 1973 he requested that I give him the English translation. But at no time during his June visit to the United States had Solzhenitsyn's representative requested of me—or, to my knowledge, of anyone else—either of the two existing English-language versions of *Gulag*. He had asked for only the Russian text, which he took away with him. Obviously, since I was not asked for the translation, I could hardly have refused on any grounds, but, in fact, far from being in an unready condition, the translation of volume one was, in June 1973, quite ready to be turned over to a publisher. And since, on that same trip, Heeb himself had met with Tom Whitney, how could I possibly have spoken for Tom?

2. Apparently, Dr. Heeb was also saying that in October 1973, having received three volumes of "translation," he assumed they were the edited version. Indeed, he was maintaining, according to the letter I now held, that he had only just now learned from Solzhenitsyn himself that the volumes he received were unedited. But how could that be? To begin with, in June 1973, while

serving lunch to the Heebs and to Tony, I myself had explained that, of the three translated volumes of *Gulag*, only one was edited and ready. And, conscious of the Swiss lawyer's imperfect English, I repeated myself yet again over coffee. Then, in September of that year, as soon as Solzhenitsyn's decision to publish *Gulag* had become known to me and with a copy of Heeb's letter requesting the Whitney translation also in hand, I had asked Tony to put "the work of [our] collective on Volume I" at Dr. Heeb's disposal and been told that Solzhenitsyn's representative did not want our version.

I put the notebook back into my purse. I was no longer angry, as I had been in Zurich, but clearly I had failed to persuade Solzhenitsyn that we were not responsible for the delay of *Gulag* in English. Before me, in Solzhenitsyn's words, was a web of accusations worthy of the most arcane subplot in the Italian Opera. I folded up the letter and put that away as well. Ordering a second café crème, I opened a manuscript and began to read. It was a memoir about my childhood, which I had begun not long before. A Paris café was a good place to work on it.

LATER THAT SPRING, Solzhenitsyn published his long autobiographical work, *How the Calf Butted the Oak*. It contains the following passage, referring to the publication in English of *Gulag*:

> Earlier, following immediately after the Russian edition, the American edition was to appear. I had done everything for it, but two or three dry, mercenary people of Western education turned everything to ashes . . . the American edition will be late by a half year, will not support me by pulling me across the chasm—and for this reason I think there was the denouement [arrest, expulsion, loss of nationality]. Yet it would have been, it could have been—conceivably the leaders giving in, if by New Year of the year 1974 all of America was really reading the book, but now in the Kremlin they only know how to weave tales to the effect that it celebrated the Hitlerites. . . .

By this time, given the "into the fire" letter and his letter to me after the Zurich meeting, this brief, accusatory reference to us came as no great surprise. I was almost beyond being hurt by it. Few readers would notice it in the existing French and Russian editions, and only our closest associates, those in the secret circle, would know who was meant.

Yet at a deeper level I was appalled by the unfairness of the charge.

In the fall, I learned that Solzhenitsyn had stated, before friends of ours, that we had been "dishonest" in our financial dealings on his account. I realized that, unless the full story was told, that false charge would also be added to the accusation of having caused his expulsion from Russia.

I realized that as future scholars assembled the story of Solzhenitsyn and his emergence into world fame, I would appear in history in a footnote, as a dry mercenary who was responsible for Alexander Solzhenitsyn's expulsion from the Soviet Union.

I set aside the memoir about my childhood. I began to sketch, in a plaid notebook, the scenes which would become the opening chapter of this book.

EIGHT

In Search of Solzhenitsyn

25

IN LATE JUNE of 1975, for several evenings at newstime, Solzhenitsyn would erupt on television into our living room in Connecticut. It was a memorable experience for me: I was thrilled
by the fact that he was making himself heard throughout the
world. At the same time I was fascinated by the further changes
in his appearance since my encounter with him only a few months
before. Stout, bearded, fierce looking, wearing a coat which was
part priest's cassock, part field jacket, he glowered and waved his
arms at the American audiences, warning them against their
weakness in the face of communism, sermonizing at them for
their blindness, predicting that the West's hour of reckoning was
closer at hand than it knew. Solzhenitsyn stood alone, as if bathed
in red twilight, pointing a prophetic finger. He had become a
riveting new figure on the international political stage.

He was now the *zek* fully emerged from obscurity. He was the man an American president had shamed himself by avoiding. He was at the zenith of his powers. Yet something about this new presence perplexed me. He was not the same man I had walked with down the dark Moscow street.

Henry, who has never met Solzhenitsyn, was impressed by his imperious presence, but also, as I was, perturbed by it.

"He *is* 'a second government.' " he said.

"And God's magic sword," I added.

I remember that we discussed the tradition of Russian writers of stature becoming moral, social, and religious spokesmen for the Russian people when, in midlife, they begin to find literature too narrow a field for their powers. Gogol, Tolstoi, and to some extent my own grandfather had followed this pattern. So had others. For them as for Solzhenitsyn, the line between performance and spiritual metamorphosis was never clear.

That fall we drove across the continent to Henry's birthplace, San Francisco. For some time we had discussed moving there, planning to live in that city for the greater part of each year. For both of us it was a symbolic trip: for Henry, a homecoming; for me, a deepening of my acquaintance with America. Unlike my husband, who had published two novels between 1970 and 1975 and had served as chairman of the Freedom to Write Committee of American P.E.N., I had little to show for those years. I had helped him with his work on behalf of imprisoned writers, but, except for the exhibit of paintings in Paris and some magazine articles, my professional life had come to a standstill. Ever since the unwieldy triangle of authority had been created in 1970, my energies had been spent on fruitless, time-consuming efforts on behalf of Solzhenitsyn's trust. I think that Henry felt I was deliberately choosing to spend much of my time away from the United States. Yet I knew that I had no choice. One of us had to participate in the Italian Opera in order to prevent both of us from becoming, paradoxically, even more deeply involved in it. My Russian background and the fact I speak Russian qualified me for this inglorious task.

Now we were trying to recreate a life together, free from the constant pressures of Solzhenitsyn's affairs. Tony was working on the last formalities of our disengagement from these.* Our drive across the United States, my first such trip, was to be a first step in this new life.

In late October we found ourselves in Cody, Wyoming. On arrival at our motel, I called our Connecticut answering service for messages. Mr. Curto had called. Would we phone him at his office in the morning? It was urgent.

We had dinner that night at the Irma Hotel, built by Buffalo Bill at the height of his fame as a showman. I was enchanted by this lively establishment, its walls ornamented with mooseheads and old photographs, its immense cherrywood bar where cowboys—or convincing facsimiles of cowboys—were served by a large, bearded bartender wearing an embroidered vest. Solzhenitsyn seemed very far away. I had put Tony's message out of mind. The next day we would be driving to Yellowstone Park, the Teton mountains.

In the morning, from a phone in the small restaurant where we were having breakfast, Henry called Tony. The call was a long one. When he came back to the table, I saw from his face that something momentous had happened.

"We're on the front page of the *New York Times Book Review*," he told me. "Patricia Blake's review of *Gulag Two* quotes Solzhenitsyn's reference to us in the *Calf*—as the mercenaries who got him thrown out of Russia."

I had last met Patricia Blake on that hot May afternoon in 1968 on which Neizvestny's opening was held. She had come up to me then urging me to prevail upon Harper & Row to stop the publication of *The First Circle* in America.

My heart sank. I had almost managed to put the accusation out of my mind; now it hit me even harder than it had before.

---

* He had also been retained directly by Solzhenitsyn to secure a settlement of IRS claims against funds transferred to Zurich.

As we drove out of Cody toward Yellowstone, we talked about what we should do, both certain now that we could not live with the accusation, that somehow we must answer it.

A makeshift sign announced that the road through Yellowstone Park and the Tetons was closed by early snows.

On the long detour to the southeast to rejoin the interstate highway west, driving through the plateau country of southern Wyoming, I realized the full impact this published proof of Solzhenitsyn's repudiation had on me. For a long time, I could not overcome the shock and remained in a kind of emotional limbo.

I began reliving the intricacies of my relationship with him, trying to understand how my efforts on his behalf could have resulted in this public accusation. I remembered Chukovsky's words about "this man who was possessed."

And now, just as Henry and I were leaving one birchwood in Connecticut, so I had left behind me those distant birches of the heart. I felt orphaned. Solzhenitsyn, whom I had served with joy and, in having done so, lost my family homeland, was now obliterating my Russian origins. I was another dry Western mercenary.

WHEN WE REACHED San Francisco, Henry found it easier than I to settle into a carefree existence in his native city. A very lonely life began for me. But in time there were interesting new acquaintances.

Some weeks after our arrival we went to a dinner party where we met Daniel Ellsberg and his wife Patricia. The conversation turned to Solzhenitsyn's *Lenin in Zurich*, which had just been published in the United States. Our host mentioned that Henry and I had helped publish *The First Circle* in the West and that I had known its author. Ellsberg, blue-eyed, young-looking, intense yet somehow distracted, was suddenly all concentration.

"Perhaps you can tell me about this man," he said. "He was one of my inspirations when I decided to release the Pentagon papers. I was facing what I consider to be a fundamental ethical question of our time—*his* question. Must an individual remain a silent accomplice to his government's crimes?

"I was still working for the Rand Corporation when I read *The First Circle*, a book I immensely admire. The atmosphere around me then was not unlike that of the scientific institute described in the novel. We weren't prisoners, of course, but we too were isolated. We had security. We loved our work. We enjoyed intellectual friendships. I identified with Solzhenitsyn and with his heroes in *The First Circle*. I even felt a parallel between our predicaments, and eventually the time came when I too had to leave the safety of my work and speak out.

"And then one day, soon after his miraculous emergence from the Soviet Union, I read in the papers that Solzhenitsyn was singling me out as a traitor to my country in time of war, a destroyer of democracy. I was shaken. To this day I am deeply affected. On what grounds was Solzhenitsyn condemning me? I had tried to emulate him. Of course I had acted in far less dangerous conditions. Nor do I mean to compare the Soviet regime with ours. And yet . . ."

Ellsberg's searching eyes, his low, passionate voice drew me back into the turmoil of the past years. As we sat down to dinner in pleasant friendly company, I remembered Solzhenitsyn in Moscow, in Zurich. My mind was racing. I thought of the contradictory faces of dissent, Russian and American, of Solzhenitsyn's condemnation of Ellsberg—of his almost fanatical belief that nothing the West did mattered except insofar as it undermined the existing Soviet regime. I found it hard to follow the light conversation at dinner.

Afterward, I spoke again with Ellsberg. Henry joined us. We discussed Solzhenitsyn's attacks against the Western press that had helped him achieve fame and immunity from imprisonment. Why had he attacked the West so violently in the original "Letter to the Soviet Leaders" and then softened the attack—omitting the treason charge against Ellsberg—in the published version meant for Western eyes? Could he really imagine now that the Soviet leaders would adopt the political alternative he proposed, a Russia without Marxist ideology?

As we talked I found myself wondering whether the Solzhenitsyn of 1976, blamed us not only his expulsion but also for the failure to change the course of Russian history.

And as always when I searched for the truth about Solzhenitsyn, the same enigma reappeared: Was he the author of *One Day* and of *The First Circle*, the man I had met in 1967, or had his sensibilities undergone some radical mutation, the effect of great personal trials, political pressures, and also of fame, of ambition, of power?

This conversation awakened many painful memories. Driving back to our apartment on Telegraph Hill, through a silvery fog filled with the sound of fog horns, I yearned once again, as I had done after the Washington march, to be an American. I longed to be free of the heavy spell which Russia and her past had cast upon my life. I wanted to belong to my husband's city. Looking at the misty necklaces of streetlights, which reminded me of those I had seen from the balcony in Moscow and which I would never see again, I suddenly knew that this sense of belonging would be mine one day, perhaps sooner than I thought. To break the spell, to heal the wound, I would need all my intelligence and all my courage. I would have to write a book that would tell the truth as completely as possible, not only about Solzhenitsyn but also about myself. Only by telling this story could I free myself to reconstruct a world of my own, where past and present, Russia and America, could be reconciled.

By early 1976 we were settled for the winter in San Francisco, and I went back to the plaid notebook in which I had begun to sketch the early scenes of this narrative. Writing the Solzhenitsyn story and its meaning to my life, I found myself searching into corners of my mind I had never approached before. The perpetual springtime of San Francisco only heightened my feeling of estrangement. I became depressed and exhilarated by turns, a moody Russian. I strove to come to terms with this emotionally difficult time in our lives, with its moments of exaltation, of frustration, of pride—and of great distress. People close to me advised me to put my experiences in the past, to forget. I would have liked to let time cool the events of almost a decade, but I found that I had to go on. It was Henry, in the course of an otherwise casual conversation one afternoon, who suggested the deepest reason for me to write this book. As we were having a cup of tea, looking out at the glorious bay dotted with white, winglike sails, Henry reminded me of what Solzhenitsyn had said in his Nobel prize address: ". . . and the simple course of the simple brave man is not to participate in the lie and not to support lying actions. Even if they come into the world and reign in the world, let it not be through me."

"I will help you to write this book in any way I can," Henry said. We were in effect to collaborate on it, as we had all along on our Solzhenitsyn mission.

On that sunny afternoon, with a sense of relief, I made a discovery which, had it not been for my years of involvement with Soviet people and Soviet situations, would have been evident to me from the first: I was free. I could tell the truth.

In the Soviet Union, with Solzhenitsyn at night near the Leningradskaya Hotel; speaking in lowered voices on a balcony; trembling in rage as an official pawed through the clothes in my suitcase; seeing friends abashed and sometimes terrified as they pointed to the ceiling: I had shared the sense of degradation which, no matter how great one's inner resources, accompanies one's *going along* with repression, one's *fitting in* to lower the odds that the secret police will pound on the door of friends, or on one's own door. I had shared their need to stifle the urge to speak truthfully, to write even coded squiggles in a pocket notebook.

Our circle was not the only network of contacts outside the USSR used by Solzhenitsyn. However it was the most dangerous to him while he was still in Russia. Against the greatest odds it had remained secret when it had to be secret—until its creator's arrival in the West. Only the guardians of Soviet repression could be outraged by the story of dedicated people on both sides of the Iron Curtain working for his original mission—truth. Perhaps this story even contains some slight promise that our divided world can in time become one.

THAT SPRING, the Russian-born pianist Vladimir Horowitz gave a concert at the Oakland Auditorium. I remember him walking on stage, making a courtly bow, sitting down at the black piano in the huge hall walled with golden art deco carvings. He looked incredibly young for his seventy-odd years. As he began to play, I felt proud to be both a Russian and an American. Russia had formed this musician; the United States had allowed him to survive and to become one of the great artists of our time.

Listening to Chopin's Ballade in G Minor, I thought with wonderment of the reaches of human possibility. I thought of Solzhenitsyn and of the uses he had made of his life. For the first time in several years I could see it whole: how from the depths of prison, from the defilement of injustice, Solzhenitsyn had fought, campaigned, marshaled his armies—his books—in a triumphal march of the spirit that would leave forever its mark on the twentieth century. As the music lifted my thoughts, I reflected upon a man who climbs so far above ordinary human experience that he is committed to the company of alien and perhaps inhospitable gods. Hearing that music, I believed that I understood Alexander Solzhenitsyn.